A VISION FOR GROWTH

Other titles by Robin Gill include:

Beyond Decline (SCM Press 1988)

Competing Convictions (SCM Press 1989)

Christian Ethics in Secular Worlds (T & T Clark 1991)

Moral Communities (Exeter University Press 1992)

The Myth of the Empty Church (SPCK 1993)

A Vision for Growth

Why your church doesn't have to be a pelican in the wilderness

Robin Gill

First published in Great Britain 1994
Society for Promoting Christian Knowledge
Holy Trinity Church
Marylebone Road
London NW1 4DU

British Library Cataloguing-in-Publication Data
A catalogue record for this book is available
from the British Library

ISBN 0-281-04759-6

Typeset by Pioneer Associates, Perthshire
Printed in Great Britain by
Biddles Ltd, Guildford and King's Lynn

Contents

Introduction

Pelicans were a recurring theme last summer. With their frying pan beaks and their angular contours, they obtruded again and again and in some unexpected places.

The first time was when Qantas ® managed to lose our tickets for 24 hours. Everything had been planned for a month-long lecture tour of Australia and Papua New Guinea. Part of my job requires me to spend the summer term lecturing and preaching in the Anglican Church world-wide. The year before it was India and Hong Kong; this year it was to be further east still—that is, until Qantas mislaid the tickets.

We wandered around central London for some time during these 24 hours to relieve the frustration. Everything was ready: the dogs had been packed off, the house made safe, the gas turned off (I think), bills paid, farewells made. Then, for a whole day, there was absolutely nothing to do . . . apart from fume.

St James's Park is always a godsend for the stranded and fuming. At the end of April, the spring flowers were fading, but the new leaves were unfolding everywhere and the birds were chattering excitedly. Time to nest, time to breed, time to bring a

1

new generation into this oasis in the centre of London's traffic.

Then, I remembered that St James's Park is famous for its black swans and that black swans come from Australia. I had seen pictures of black swans gracing the Botanic Gardens in Melbourne. So, even if we could not get to Melbourne, we could at least pretend that we were there for a few moments. Naturally, the leaves in Melbourne would be turning autumnal, but the temperature would be similar.

Then, the pelicans obtruded. Trying to admire the black swans, we found, instead, that we were watching the antics of the ridiculous pelicans. Some were noisily defending their nests in the centre of the lake, while others were snoozing ostentatiously with their heads swivelled over their backs. Others again were pleading for bread from the tourists—a loaf at a time to fill those beaks—despite the many notices clearly telling them not to beg for food. Whereas the black swans glided past with their heads and necks held proudly in an S-shape, the pelicans paddled past maintaining a less than elegant Z-shape.

A peculiar creature, stranded in central London. Angular and out of place. Lovable, perhaps, and not without its own fascination, but not quite matching the elegance of the black swan. Is that an apt image of the church at the moment?

I decided there and then that I would write a book about pelicans . . . I mean about the churches in Britain today. Have churches become pelicans? And if they have, is there anything that Christians can do about this?

For a number of years, I have been studying churches. Some of my work has been highly statistical.

In *The Myth of the Empty Church*, and, earlier, in *Competing Convictions*, I mapped out churchgoing patterns in Britain for the last 170 years. From this, I tried to identify some of the factors producing the decline in churchgoing. Some people enjoyed these statistics, but others, I am afraid, found that they merely obscured the point I was making. In this book, I promise that there will be almost no statistics.

Other parts of my work have been in highly technical areas of Christian ethics. The modern social sciences and physical sciences are throwing up many fresh ethical and theological issues. In a number of books, I have attempted to explore several of these, but I am going to leave technicalities to one side here. This is meant to be a practical book; those who want footnotes and technicalities can read these other books.

This work has convinced me that churches in Britain need to make urgent choices about structure and direction. If they are to cease being pelicans, they need to be much clearer about how they might be effective in present-day Britain. They need to be more single-minded about growth . . . about how they might reach the nine out of ten people in Britain who seldom or never go to church.

The tickets turned up next day. Airlines dare not admit to failure—that might prove expensive. Instead, they admitted only to a functional delay. However, at least now we could fly.

Perth first, then Melbourne. The Botanic Gardens were splendid. The black swans were positively stately, and if there were any pelicans, they kept discreetly hidden. Instead, they appeared in the liturgy. In the midst of worship, we were informed, 'My heart is smitten down and withered like grass: so that

3

I forget to eat my bread. For the voice of my groaning: my bones will scarce cleave to my flesh. I am become like a pelican in the wilderness' (Psalm 102).

Looking at churches in Britain today, it is not difficult to spot pelicans in the wilderness. Vast, Victorian church buildings can be found stranded in many urban wildernesses: neo-Gothic architecture that has seen better days; discoloured stone or brickwork, windows caged against vandalism, and doors kept firmly locked on weekdays to prevent theft. On Sundays, congregations are scarce, the organ may or may not be working, and there may be no children in the choir, nor even a Sunday school. Many churches serve a dwindling number of aged people and are visited by others just about as often as they visit pelicans.

Or else it is exquisite medieval churches dotted thickly over rural Britain. For more than a hundred years the population of Britain has been predominantly urban. Yet the Church of England, the Church of Scotland, the English Methodist Church, and several Welsh Churches still have a majority of their churches in the countryside. A notice in the porch may tell visitors where the key can be obtained, and that once a month there will be a service. The nearest vicar or minister is several parishes distant, and the local Baptist or Congregational chapel is now an antique shop. A church-going population has been replaced by horse-boxes and summer tourists.

Churches have gradually ceased to be places of worship and have become curious pelicans instead. Exotic things to marvel at on holiday—a bit like the comforting flock of pelicans at the end of the film *Jurassic Park*.

Until recently, I looked after a church myself. For 20 years, while working as a full-time academic, I looked after a series of inner urban and rural churches in my spare time. Now I travel around preaching in other people's churches. Everywhere I go, I spot these pelicans—in England, Scotland and Wales, even in Australia, they are everywhere.

When we got to Cairns, they were there as well. This time they were in the wild, although still not exactly in the wilderness. They were paddling in a scruffy, untidy group up and down the sea front, just out from the muddy beach. Looking as awkward as ever, they clashed incongruously with the sleek vessels carrying tourists to the barrier reef. To make matters worse, they were feeding on colourful fish that looked as if they had just escaped from a tropical fish tank. I suppose at least they were not begging from the tourists.

The human beings did that instead. For a mere 40 dollars, you could buy a cut-out wooden pelican and hang it from a string so its wings would flap in the wind. Tempting stuff.

Of course, there are some important exceptions. In this book I look closely at a number of these . . . at churches that are still growing. As I travel around the world, I hear of some startling church growth in parts of South-East Asia, and I see some growing churches in Britain, too. Yet, the tough question I wish to ask in this book is this: can churches as a whole grow in static, apathetic Britain today?

Church growth is certainly possible when populations are mobile and growing. South-East Asia shows that at the moment, and Britain showed it in the nineteenth century, but is overall church growth possible when populations are static? Even worse, is such growth possible when (as so often in Europe) populations are apathetic as well as static? The troubling evidence I will examine is that examples of church growth in Britain today are still set in an overall context of a decline in churchgoing.

Granted this, what would we have to do if we were going to turn a majority of pelicans into swans? It is not enough to have lots of pelicans and a few swans. In a way, the few swans just make the many pelicans look even more absurd. Growth is really only growth when most churches are swans not pelicans. Much as I like pelicans, I find it difficult to take them seriously. Perhaps that is also a problem for many Britons today.

Lurking behind these questions are a number of assumptions that must be justified at an early point in this book. There is an assumption, for a start, that numbers of churchgoers matter and that empty churches *are* pelicans. Many would argue, instead, that it is the job of a church simply to be there, whether or not anyone comes to it; pelicans do not have to *do* anything.

There is, too, an assumption that something can be done to change the present churchgoing situation in Britain. Many argue instead that things may change eventually but, in the meantime, there is little that we can do but survive as best we can. History rolls on, and there is little that human beings can do to change it, and, in any case, it is for God to change the church. Things will change in God's good time. The Spirit blows where it will . . .

Near Darwin, we finally did find pelicans in the wilderness—even if it was a controlled wilderness. Half an hour out from Darwin, there is a splendid wildlife park. It was a hot afternoon, so several exotic marsupials refused to make an appearance. A large notice assured us that they were there even if we could not see them. Yet, frankly, the difference between an enclosure with a hidden marsupial and an enclosure that is simply empty is not great—a bit like a church, perhaps?

Finally, we came to the pelicans. By this time we had developed a firm affection for pelicans. At 3.30pm, they were to be fed, so we timed our arrival carefully. A keeper came with buckets of raw fish, and children were invited to chuck them out to the pelicans. The pelicans responded by catching the fish lazily in their great beaks and then dropping them, uneaten, into the water. 'I am afraid they are just not hungry', the keeper apologized. The pelicans ignored this truism: they continued to beg, the children continued to throw, they, in turn, continued to catch and then simply to drop.

Over-fed pelicans still *look* hungry, they just do not do anything much with the food. They beg, they catch, but they do not actually eat. A most peculiar bird. Awkward, out of place, angular, with a big mouth but little brain, demanding but inactive, and outshone by the swan at every turn.

One of the difficulties for churches is that there is something quite comfortable about being pelicans, particularly in well-controlled wildlife parks or even in St James's Park. There is enough food to survive, even if overall numbers keep dwindling slowly. There is certainly enough food to see us out and being a pelican is at least different. Not as elegant as the swan, of course, but, none the less, distinctive. Naturally, pelicans do not change the world, but then they probably do not expect to. They just paddle along, surviving and looking peculiar and lovable.

Strangers in the world. Incongruous birds to be found in a limited number of unexpected locations. Not a bad life perhaps . . . for a bird at least, but not much of a role for churches.

Even if it is agreed that something ought to be done to change the present situation, there is little agreement about *what* exactly should be done. Some believe that effective preaching is a priority: first, we must win people's minds and turn them to Christ, then we can expect them to come back to church. Others (including myself) believe, quite oppositely, that belonging usually *precedes* belief and that structural questions are crucial. There is much to be unravelled here in the central chapters of this book.

Even the most dedicated church growth enthusiast might admit that numerical growth is not everything. Somehow, if churches are to cease being pelicans, they must seek to influence the world. More and more pelicans would just produce . . . more and more pelicans. They need something else. They need to win the affection of people beyond the churches and to influence their lives, whether or not others choose to belong. Values and care need to spread outwards deep into society at large (this is a crucial theme in the final chapter).

Involved in all of this is a vision of something else. Yet, visions have a habit of never being transformed into reality—they become just another impossible dream for the churches, one more voice giving unhelpful criticism and advice. In contrast, I hope that what follows is thoroughly grounded in things that could be done. We need the will to do them, of course. We do need the vision to give this will direction. Indeed. However, we also need enough practical wisdom to carry this vision out.

I have tried to make this book as practical as possible. A number of friends have helped me to do this by reading earlier drafts. Norman Baldock, John Court, and John Craven have all given valuable help in this way and Ted Harrison has added his splendid drawings. To all of them, many, many thanks. My only possible excuse for adding yet another book to bookshop shelves is that critical ideas from the scholarly world do need to be translated into practical remedies for the churches at large.

CHAPTER 1
Starting with God

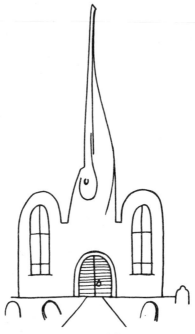

There is a fable that goes as follows.

A seeker after truth puzzled about the difference between pelicans and churches, so she went to a person of facts, to a person of deep thought, and, finally, to a person of God.

'What is the difference between pelicans and churches?', she asked the person of facts.

'Don't be silly', replied the person of facts. 'Pelicans are living creatures. They eat, drink, breathe, and reproduce. They have feathers and large mouths. They are to be found in zoos and wildlife parks or out in the wild in hot countries, whereas churches are inanimate buildings made of bricks or stone. They cannot reproduce, without the help of human beings. They do not eat, drink or breathe (although some people do say that they eat up money). They are not to be found either in zoos or in wildlife parks. They can be found in the wild, but are also sometimes found in places where people live. Churches and pelicans are usually very different from each other.'

The seeker after truth thought that this was a very clear answer, yet it puzzled her because she had heard churches being compared with pelicans. What could this mean? So, she went to a person of deep thought.

'What is the difference between pelicans and churches?', she asked.

'Now, there is an interesting question', replied the person of deep thought. 'But it is not an easy question to answer. The trouble is that pelicans and churches both come in animate and in inanimate varieties. The word 'church' can sometimes refer to a building, it can sometimes refer to people who are Christians, and it can sometimes refer to a denomination. It can even indicate a practice—as in sentences about people going to church. By this we usually mean, not that people simply go to a church building, or even go into a church building, but that they go to take part in a service held within a church building. All very different meanings for one word. The meanings for the word 'pelican' are almost as numerous. For example, as well as birds, there are pelican crossings that, to my knowledge, neither look like birds nor act as crossings for pelican birds. Pelicans and churches can be very different and they can also be quite similar.'

The seeker was just as puzzled by this answer, so she went to the person of God.

'What is the difference between pelicans and churches?', she asked.

'The answer rests in the intentions of the creator', replied the person of God. 'God made pelicans for fun, but God made churches for worship.'

Of course, this *is* a fable.

There is something decidedly odd about claiming that God made pelicans for fun. Why not sparrows or owls? And, in any case, what about Darwinian theories of evolution? Some claim that they strip God of any special intentions. As a result, pelicans become just quirks of evolution.

There may, also, be something bewildering about claiming that God made churches for worship. Everyone knows that you do not *need* church buildings (I will opt for that understanding of 'church' for the moment) in order to worship. Everyone knows, too, that church buildings spend most of their lives *not* providing space for worship—an hour or two every Sunday, if they are lucky. For most of the week, they are just empty buildings. Only if they are very famous or beautiful are they used by tourists as places to visit. A flood of tourists equivalent to about half of the population of England visited its cathedrals and churches last year . . . but not for worship.

However, it is a starting point that can be refined later. The idea is simply that the primary object of a church (in any sense of the word) is to encourage the worship of God. Church buildings were built in the first place to provide places for worship, not to become historic buildings for sightseers. Churches as denominations have worship as the primary objective. They go to great lengths to provide ministers and buildings all over the country so that worship is available for all. And churches as people are people who gather together at regular intervals to worship God in Christ.

Whenever I go to conferences to talk about strategies for church growth, there are always two people in the audience. I am almost convinced that they are the same two people who follow me around the country.

I always (well, perhaps, if I am really honest, nearly always) make a point of starting with God. My understanding of church growth starts from worship; it is theologically based. Yet, when I have finished speaking after the usual 55 minutes—most university teachers are conditioned to speak for that length of time—a rather aggressive hand always goes up. And exactly the same question follows each time: 'When are you going to bring God into all of this?'

A mixture of points follow this rhetorical question. Some of them go straight to the Holy Ghost—less often to the Holy Spirit. If I truly believed in the Holy Ghost, I would not worry about strategies for church growth, or, indeed, about strategies for anything very much.

This person will sometimes battle with the whole of sociology, or, even worse, with all management theories. Thatcherism is frequently mentioned—I think more in the context of management theories than the Holy Ghost. Just the mention of the word Thatcherism is usually sufficient to show that everything I have said for the preceding 55 minutes is rubbish. Academic rubbish, perhaps, but rubbish none the less.

The other person to object is much more languorous. Typically, one ankle is placed on the other thigh, hands are interlocked behind the neck, and the ubiquitous plastic chair is at a 45 degree angle. So far, this person has never tipped over, but he does always go straight for the anatomy: 'Why do you keep going on about bums on seats?'

Frankly, I never mention xxxx on seats, except, of course, in reported speech. I was much too well brought up for that. I even remember using French euphemisms for bottoms in school. xxxx is just not a part of my usual vocabulary. Yet, this chap—it is always a chap—keeps bringing them up (or is it down?), whenever I speak.

So, why am I so obsessed? It is true that I spend my life studying churchgoing figures from all over the country. I ransack historical records, and I am the despair of county archivists in many parts of Britain.

Why am I so obsessed that, when I speak for those 55 minutes, this man in the audience gets so annoyed with my findings that he forgets that I started with God? My obsessions get such predictable reactions that you would think that I might learn one day. Learn simply to forget about all this church growth stuff. Learn to accept decline like everyone else.

Why not leave it up to God instead? Things will become better or worse (according to your perspective) one day. There is absolutely nothing for us to do in the meantime, whatsoever. In any case, is it really very likely that British churches—and the Church of England in particular—will change their ways? Radical reform is just a dream. Forget it.

So why?

The answer is surprisingly simple. If worship is the primary object of the church, then it should be a matter of concern to Christians that fewer and fewer people in Britain worship.

Naturally this answer needs some unpacking. Perhaps I can start slightly sideways. There is, I believe, an important link between worship and God-talk.

Has it ever struck you as strange that we can talk meaningfully about God at all? If God really is the Creator of all that is, how can mere creatures believe that their creaturely language can adequately signify the mysteries of the Creator? I guess an ant might find it quite difficult to talk meaningfully to another ant about the human mind. Even while crawling over a human skull—on the way to being swiped by a human hand—there may not be too much that an ant knows about what goes on inside that skull. Yet many people think that they can talk meaningfully about the mind of God.

If God really is God, then God-talk must always be a problem. For the most part, what human beings do is stretch everyday language when talking about God. God is a great king. Well not exactly a king in any human sense—neither a despotic monarch of Tudor times nor a constitutional monarch of the late twentieth century. No. The image of God as king is meant to convey something of the importance of God, something about the way that God 'works' in the world.

God is love. Well, yes. Yet we know most about love from other human beings: the love of parents for their children, the love of two lovers, the love of people for animals, the love of saints caring for those otherwise unloved. All are powerful images of love, but none quite measures up to the claim that

God is love. God is *all*-loving. Not just very loving, not just very, very, very loving, but all-loving. Language is taken to breaking point. A human term is applied to God only with some difficulty.

The word 'holy' is an exception. For once, the rules are reversed. It is God who is depicted first and foremost as holy. People are depicted as holy only because they seem to be more God-like than the rest of us. A saint is seen as holy because her holiness has some relation to God's holiness. There is a mysterious quality about the saint that we call holiness.

Normally, language works the other way around. Terms are taken from the human context, stretched very considerably, and then applied to God who is, in truth, beyond these terms.

Some people of faith have concluded from this that we really should not talk about God at all; silence should be used to depict God. Others have argued that only negative terms can be used when talking about God—God is *not* evil, God is *not* limited, and so forth. Yet, frankly, it is very difficult to follow either of these paths consistently. It is important to be reminded about the inappropriateness of human language, yet most people of faith do wish to avoid perpetual silence or endless negatives. Most of us want to say something more positively about God.

Therein lies the problem. How can we speak meaningfully about God while still using human language?

I am convinced that the answer lies in worship. It is in worship especially that we find ourselves prompted to move beyond silence or negatives. It was in worship that some of the earliest Christians first used divine language about Christ. It was in worship that some of our creeds were fashioned. It is in worship that we use psalms and hymns—with their rich language about God. It is in worship that Scripture lives and takes on fresh resonances. It is in worship that God-talk becomes especially meaningful. This is the primary context for this language. In worship, we share God-talk together, even when, as individuals, we only half understand it.

There is a second link to be made. Worship links not just to God-talk, but also to values. Worship has strong implications for Christian living and morality. Worshipping communities carry and sustain values that may be only half realized by individual worshippers.

At the moment, there is much discussion—and also much confusion—about the relation between values and churches. I will return to this and discuss it in greater detail in Chapter 6, but here I shall just dispel a few misunderstandings.

Whenever there is a particularly brutal murder or an outbreak of vandalism, it is commonplace for some politicians to blame the church. 'Churches have gone soft on sin', they cry. 'Once upon a time, churches used to teach people right from wrong.' 'Church leaders should spend less time trying to meddle in politics, and more time instilling moral values into people.' 'Why can't churches get back to their proper role in the nation—training young people to lead decent lives?'

Alliterations abound in many of the tabloid newspapers—'barmy bishops', 'mad monks', 'prattling prelates', 'meddlesome ministers'—though I have yet to spot vacuous vicars or even 'orrible ordinands. Somehow a link is made between the increase in crime, the demise of the family, and the soft liberalism of the churches. They become fused together.

The solution is, therefore, for the churches to take sin seriously again. Then, the nation will, presumably, respond, turn back to God, and encourage people to be hard-working, honest and sexually faithful.

There is just about enough truth in all of this to sustain these links. Nevertheless, they are gross over-simplifications. The high rates of churchgoing in the United States, together with high crime and divorce rates, should make this much obvious. Yet, having said that, there may well be a greater link between worshipping communities and moral values in society at large than some intellectuals have allowed.

In worship, we do not simply invent values or agree to abide by social contracts; we are confronted with an array of stories, parables, and teaching that are soaked in Christian values. These are part of the data of churchgoing. They are there whether we want them to be there or not. Central notions of forgiveness, of acting beyond self-regarding interest, of concern for the disadvantaged, and of unmerited grace, are recurrent themes in worship. They are embedded in the prayers, in the hymns, and, above all, in the New Testament readings that sustain Christian worship.

In worship, we are heirs to a store-room of values stocked by the earliest Christians who knew Jesus in the flesh. We are heirs to a tradition that has been expounded and interpreted (doubtless in many differing ways) by Christian communities over two millennia. Inevitably, we are shaped by all of this in ways that may now be largely invisible to us. We are moulded by our long history, shared together in our worship. We are part of a unbroken community reaching back to the figure of Jesus.

In short, worship carries and sustains values. Christians may not always exemplify these values. Sadly, we know that this is all too often the case. Yet Christians are (as I shall argue at length in Chapter 6) still heirs to these values. The worshipping communities to which Christians belong carry these values relentlessly from one generation to another.

Of course, I am not claiming that the primary role of worship is to sustain values. No, the primary role of worship is to worship God. Any effect that worship may have on us is secondary to that. It is not a mechanism designed to keep unthinking people in good moral order. Or, to express this in blunter Marxist terms, it is not a system that is designed by the élite to keep the masses firmly under control. Perhaps some politicians still view the churches in that way. For most worshippers, however, that would be a hopeless misunderstanding of their worship.

No, most Christians worship in order to worship God in Christ. God is, indeed, the starting point. Over the centuries Christians have gone to considerable trouble to provide church buildings and resident priests and ministers in order to sustain worship as worship, not worship as a means to something else.

If worship of God is at the centre of Christian worship, then the moral life may flow out from this worship. The moral life is not the main object of worship, but it should be a fruit of it. Worship has the power to change lives. Those who worship usually do so in the belief that, in worship, we touch the deepest level of reality. We come into the very presence of the Creator. When we share bread and wine together, we share in the very life of Christ; the risen Christ is present with us in the Eucharist. And at the conclusion of the Eucharist, we are invited each time to become new people and go forth in the name of Christ.

Since Christian worship contains within it so many deep moral values, it is hardly surprising to discover some links here. For example, there is a measurable link between worshippers and moral action in the community. In a growing number of surveys, it appears that those who are both churchgoers *and* Christian believers are highly likely to be involved in voluntary care in the community. Conversely, the person who is least likely to be involved in such care is the one who never goes to church and who disavows all religious belief.

Naturally, there are important exceptions to this. We can doubtless all think of individuals who are deeply caring and yet who are declared atheists or agnostics. Equally, it is not difficult to spot professing Christians who seldom do anything much to help others. Caring beyond self-regarding interest is not the monopoly of Christians. Yet, on balance, it does seem to be the case that Christians are represented rather generously among voluntary carers.

To make matters even more confusing, Christians are often encouraged not to boast about their 'good works'. If they are involved in care, then they are encouraged to do this humbly and without trying to claim any personal credit. They are also told to be sensitive to those other carers who do not share their Christian faith. Not surprisingly, it is common for analysts to underestimate the extent of the specifically Christian care that goes on in a community.

The church has sometimes been pictured as a human body. The torso is worship—after all, it contains the heart, stomach, and lungs. It receives nourishment from outside, and, in turn, pumps life-giving blood around the rest of the body. The right arm is social action—caring action in the community. Sustained by worship, the right arm is the church engaged in the world, the church sharing its values with the world, the church caring beyond self-regarding interest.

The left arm is mission or outreach. If worship is the torso, the provider of life-giving blood, then mission is the attempt to draw more people into this worship. Effective social action depends on there being sufficient numbers of people to sustain it. As a result, mission is inevitably concerned with how many people do, in fact, worship in any society.

To reduce all of this to numbers simply as numbers and nothing else is absurd. My concern has never been about 'numbers' coming to worship; it is about *people* coming to worship. If worship is treated as central in an understanding of the church, then the fact that fewer and fewer people worship in Britain today (less than a third of the proportion of Victorians who worshipped regularly) has very serious implications. It is not simply a question of sustaining nice church buildings or increasing the market share of a particular denomination. Instead, it is a conviction that worship needs people and that people need to worship.

Worship is something that we do together. Of course prayer is important. It seems that many people who no longer go to church continue to pray. I know some nonchurchgoers who are people of deep and sustained prayer. Without denying this, it none the less seems to be true that this group is slowly vanishing, too. As fewer and fewer people worship, so fewer and fewer engage in anything other than fleeting and occasional prayer. Prayer becomes a last resort—worth trying if everything else has failed in a confusing world.

Such fleeting prayer is likely to remain at about play-school level, which, perhaps, is not too surprising. Sustained private prayer does need to be nourished if it is to continue and develop. It is easily excluded in busy lives. For many, too, it can become empty and wooden—'I just felt that I was talking to myself', is a complaint that is often heard.

In worship, we worship together. We *share* prayers and hymns. We listen *together* to the words of Scripture and to sermons based on that Scripture. We confess our sins regularly and we offer thanks in psalms and singing. If, in private prayer, we are left to our own devices, in worship we can be challenged by the unexpected. Lurking within worship are the thoughts and prayers of Christians passed down through the centuries. Within worship there is a ceaseless accumulation of Christian data.

If all of this is important, then mission should not be ignored. Mission is the attempt to reach out and to draw others in. This is never going to be an easy task in apathetic, static Britain. After generations of Christian preaching and ministry, Christian mission hardly represents a novelty. In the chapters that follow, I will explore this problem further, but it is the imperative to mission that is my concern here.

Reaching out is not just a specialized task for the few. It is not just a task for Evangelicals. It is a task for all. Only when the British churches see this imperative clearly can they hope to make the sort of changes that I shall be suggesting later.

All of this starts from God. It assumes that God is the primary object of worship. It assumes that the primary task of the churches is to worship. It assumes that worship makes God-talk possible and that worship encourages and sustains Christian living and values. From all of this, it concludes that the attempt to draw more people into worship is an imperative for the churches. Without mission, worship slowly fades away. Like the pelican in the wilderness.

CHAPTER 2

Believing and Belonging

Once, I let the Roman Catholic Church down badly. It was entirely unintentional, but it taught me about the power of belonging.

I was a curate in Rugby at the time. In those days, there were still six churches in the parish and six curates. It was one of the last of the celebrated training parishes in the country. The Rector was the remarkable Dilwyn Davies. Twice our age, he managed to persuade most of his curates that, politically, he was considerably to our left, while, at the same time, being an active Mason. He was vivacious and brimming with character, outshining us all with sheer exuberance.

I knew that I wanted to be one of his curates after our first meeting with him. Recently married and soon to be ordained, I went to see the splendid Cuthbert Bardsley, then Bishop of Coventry. 'Dilwyn might need another curate. Go and see him in Rugby', was the advice of this great actor Bishop. So, we knocked on the rectory door in Rugby.

'Do come in', Dilwyn gushed. Never one for listening very carefully, he was half-way through his wedding interview when he realized that we were already married and that I was actually looking for a curacy.

'My dear boy, you *must* come here, I am desperate. The Bishop *knows* that I am desperate—how could he possibly think that I *might* need a curate? *Silly* old Cuthbert!' (He always emphasised at least one word in every sentence.)

We were not yet quite convinced. We had already visited one very serious-minded and 'sensible' parish. In those days, prospective curates could pick and choose their parish. So, astutely as it turned out, Dilwyn took us to evensong at one of the six churches, Holy Trinity. This vast, Gilbert Scott church was erected next door to the parish church. The two churches were separated by nothing but the graveyard. Not surprisingly, this great High Church pelican struggled to have any congregation at all. Now demolished, even then it lacked any obvious function.

There were six other people in the congregation

that night, spaced out evenly at the edges of the church. We were placed at the front. The service was without surprises until the sermon. Then, Dilwyn preached one of the most brilliant and hilarious sermons that I had ever heard. The tiny congregation was convulsed with laughter. I knew at once that I had much to learn from a man with such remarkable skills of communication. Rugby was to be my life for the next three years.

Despite constant humour, there was a structured discipline to the life of the staff. Fridays, in particular, were always demanding. We all had to be in the hospital chapel for a service at 5.45am and then on to the wards at 6.15am giving Communion to the patients. Since the youth club invariably met the night before, I was always exhausted by Friday afternoon, and that, I am afraid, is how I came to let the Roman Catholics down so badly.

As a newly qualified doctor, my wife had taken a house job in Coventry at a very Catholic hospital. Broken nights were frequent and the work was very exacting. If she was on call over the weekend, I would visit her there in any free moments. One Friday, I arrived to find that she, too, was exhausted, yet she was to be on duty again for the next two nights. We decided to get some sleep. So, despite the fact that it was the middle of the afternoon, we climbed into her single bed and went straight to sleep.

The predictable happened. It was, of course, the day the window cleaners came and I had left my dog collar on. The door burst open. We sat up in bed. 'Aaah, sorry Father!', exclaimed a very Irish voice, and the door shut briskly.

Now, there is not much one can do in these

circumstances. Pursuing the window cleaner down the corridor would clearly have been undignified—especially as I was not fully dressed. He might or might not believe the subtle differences between Anglican and Roman Catholic forms of ministry. He certainly would not believe them from someone wearing only a dog collar and underwear. In any case, we did not have our marriage certificate conveniently to hand.

After half an hour of strangled laughter, and not a little embarrassment, we decide to go downstairs for tea. It was at that moment that we discovered all about belonging. At the foot of the stairs, the window cleaners, seemingly from the whole of Coventry, had assembled. Clearly in the middle of telling the great story, they froze when they saw us. We smiled limply and passed by. Any credibility that the local Catholic priesthood might have had, had now been destroyed. We had confirmed their worst suspicions.

Because they belonged to the same community, they believed what they saw. It was obvious. These young women doctors were perfectly capable of misleading young Catholic priests. 'Sorry Father', after all, had more than one meaning. Hospitals are famous for that sort of thing, and here was a blatant and shameless example.

On the other hand, we belonged, too, but differently. Our two worlds of belonging stared at each other in amazement. Any explanation was likely to confuse matters even further. Our beliefs and expectations were moulded by our different belongings. We were, to use the cliché, worlds apart.

In matters of faith, belonging is primary. Intellectuals are apt to forget this. We are so concerned with thought that we frequently convince ourselves that *belief* is primary. People believe and then they belong, so it is assumed . . . in that order. In contrast, I am convinced that the order is mostly the other way around—we belong and *then* we believe.

Let me return to the two critics who follow me so remorselessly around the conference circuit. They both tend to start with belief and regard belonging as very much a secondary matter. The 'bums on seats' objection is obviously contemptuous about an approach that starts from belonging. But then so is the 'when are you going to bring God into all of this' approach. It usually assumes that the first task of mission is to convince people about belief. Only once people are properly converted, will they then start going to church. Conversion is primary.

Indeed, in discussions about mission I am conscious of an argument that runs as follows. 'If you really love Jesus, everything else will follow. It is no use encouraging people to come to church in the hope that they might become Christians. First, you must convince them about the love of Jesus. It must burn through your life. It must fill your language. Once people see this, then they will respond. When they respond and make a commitment to Christ, then, and only then, will they start to become active Christians.'

There is something rather attractive about this argument. It is used (albeit in different forms) by both of my critics. The one leaning back on his plastic chair will tend to assume that it is social action that will convince people about the love of Christ. There is no difference between mission and social action; the two are identical—social action *is* mission. It is the church engaged in the world, the church demonstrating the love of Christ to others. How people respond is up to them. It is enough that the church should be seen to be there, deeply embedded in care and showing in action the love of Christ.

The more earnest critic is usually concerned instead about conversion. The way to change the world is through street evangelism—going into the market-place and accosting total strangers, engaging them in talk about Jesus, telling them about the love that Jesus has for them, assuring them of the salvation that awaits them if only they will repent and turn to Christ. Social action is largely a waste of time in terms of evangelism. It converts nobody. Conversion is brought about by confronting individuals with the truth of the Gospel.

What is seldom realized is that the assumption shared by both of these approaches—namely that Christian belonging comes later in the Christian life —is testable. One obvious way to test it would be to interview those who have recently become active Christians and also those who have recently lapsed. What would this tell us about the order of belonging and belief?

Fortunately, work on this has already been done. In the 1960s, the Methodists were particularly worried about declining membership levels. So they commissioned a series of surveys to investigate the factors behind this decline. Having completed these surveys, they then deposited them in archives in Manchester and ignored them.

The most impressive of these surveys collected together information nationally, based on several hundred interviews with lapsed members (as they were rather quaintly termed). The ministers collecting this data were asked to look at the reasons those who had lapsed gave for no longer going to church.

Surprisingly, only two of those surveyed mentioned a loss of faith as the reason for their lapsing. Most simply reported something along the lines of 'I seem to have lost interest'. Another very common reason given was that they had moved to a new area and had then failed to establish themselves in a new congregation. A mixture of apathy and mobility was a recurrent theme in the interviews, but *not* a crisis of belief. As the late 1960s was widely thought to be a time shaped by theological ferment—especially after *Honest to God* (SCM Press 1963) and the Second Vatican Council—this finding was largely unexpected.

In another survey, one industrious minister at this time went around the clubs, pubs and bingo halls in the Rhondda Valley—hardly familiar stomping ground for a Methodist minister. He went armed with copies of a brief questionnaire and succeeded in getting well over a thousand completed.

His sampling technique was scarcely wonderful—it was gloriously do-it-yourself—but, nevertheless, he did produce some fascinating results. As might have been predicted, even in Wales, only about one person in every five interviewed was a regular churchgoer. However, four out of five had been to Sunday school as children, and most still showed considerable affection for churches and chapels (and doubtless some surprise at this new role for their minister). Not one of those interviewed mentioned disbelief as the reason for not going to church now.

Naturally, this evidence on its own is not conclusive. Perhaps people were reluctant to admit their unbelief to a minister. Perhaps, too, questionnaires are not the best way of finding out what people disbelieve deep down. Yet, when this evidence is set alongside other surveys that reverse the question, it does become more convincing.

For example, when those who have recently started being active Christians are questioned, belief is seldom mentioned as the starting point of their new Christian life. What becomes very clear is that most people who come to faith do so over a period of time. Many, in fact, are returning to a faith they once knew as children. Typically, they are encouraged to start going back to church by a friend or by a member of the family. Perhaps it is a child going to Sunday school, or a son or daughter being confirmed. Perhaps it is marrying into a churchgoing family. Perhaps it is a friend who encourages them to come to church after a bereavement or after serious illness. Perhaps it is simply the desire to have new friends after moving house.

Whatever. The evidence suggests that people seldom become active Christians solely as a result of an isolated conversion experience. Of course, there are always some who report that they do and I suspect that they may be rather over-represented among clergy. The typical pattern seldom involves an intellectual conversion to faith followed by a change of religious practice. If there is a conversion experience at all, it is usually preceded by a great deal of belonging and half believing.

All of this fits the mass of statistical data that I accumulated in *The Myth of the Empty Church* very closely. This data suggested that, in England at least, Christian *belonging* started to decline long before Christian *belief*. The Church of England in urban areas has been experiencing a process of slow decline in churchgoing since about the 1850s. The

Free Churches have been experiencing a very similar process since the 1880s.

Yet, an extensive survey of Christian belief conducted by Army chaplains at the end of the First World War suggested that most of the young soldiers still believed in afterlife, in prayer and in the existence of God. They were less clear about more Christ-centred beliefs. Few of them went to church voluntarily as adults, yet most had once attended a Sunday school. A number of other surveys made just after the Second World War presented a very similar picture.

It has only been in the last 30 years or so that there has been any measurable decline in *belief* (particularly belief in afterlife) in the population at large. Also, only in the most recent surveys have young people *without* a belief in God begun to outnumber those who *do* express such a belief (in older age groups a decisive majority still believes in God).

Putting these two sets of information together, it would appear that Christian belief has persisted longer than churchgoing patterns. A major reason for this—and I will return to this point in a moment—may have been the persistence of Sunday schools. Until the 1950s, a majority of children went to a Sunday school of one denomination or another. Today, most do not. A collapse in belonging has been followed (not preceded) by a gradual decline in belief.

Of course, Christian literature is soaked in the idea that people can unexpectedly see blinding lights that change their whole life; the idea that an individual who has no faith at all, and no intention of practising any form of religion, can suddenly be 'converted'. One moment he or she is a secularist, or even a despiser of religion, and the next moment a person of faith. On this understanding, the task of mission is first and foremost to convert people, to change their minds and hearts radically, and then to wean them on to a habit of regular churchgoing.

St Paul and St Augustine are both treated as the archetypes for this approach to mission. Both are portrayed as Christians who had a profound conversion experience; one moment they were not Christians, and the next they were. Also, having become true Christian believers, they slowly became strong practising Christians as well. Conversion came first in their lives, while belonging followed later.

For some time, I have regarded this account of St Paul and St Augustine as flawed. It plays down the extent to which both seem to have been passionately religious men long before their conversions. Of course, their own writings tended to play this down, too. Perhaps it is a tendency of many people who make such profound shifts to underestimate their earlier lives.

I first became aware of this as a teenager. Attending the occasional mission rally, I was always fascinated by the lurid tales of some of those who gave 'testimonies'. A recurrent feature of such rallies was that individuals would try to outdo each other in their attempt to show just how wicked they had been before their conversion. Once they were endlessly sinful, yet, now that they had been saved, their lives had totally changed.

St Augustine's *Confessions* provided a pattern that has been copied (consciously or unconsciously) in many subsequent confessions and testimonies. Before he became an orthodox Christian, St Augustine maintained that his life was a morass of sex, sin, and superstition. Then it changed totally.

In reality, the change may not have been quite so dramatic as St Augustine portrayed. Many scholars today believe that he had *always* been earnest and deeply religious. Even his famous sex life was conventional by the standards of the class of Roman citizen to which his family belonged. Certainly he changed, but probably not quite as dramatically as he suggested. Similarly, perhaps, with St Paul. He, too, seems to have been a deeply religious person (even a fanatically religious person) long before he became a Christian.

The typical pattern instead seems to be this. Changing from unbelief to belief is usually a slow process. Sometimes it can take many years. There may have to be years of belonging before belief feels fully comfortable. Conversely, people who *stop* belonging may retain core Christian beliefs for many years—possibly for the rest of their lives. Disbelief does not appear usually to be the main reason for ceasing to go to church. Indeed, elements of Christian belief may persist long after formal Christian activity has ceased. However, what this belief will tend to be is rather uninformed belief; belief that is, in effect, frozen in time.

Perhaps this explains some of the sharp criticisms that David Jenkins has received as Bishop of Durham. Among his severest critics have been those on the edges of churches—marginal churchgoers, as they are sometimes rather rudely termed. Marginal, or occasional, churchgoers may attend at Christmas and even at Easter, but seldom at other times. Such people often remain convinced of the general 'truth' of Christian belief and strongly uphold the Christian ethic (note the singular). Above all, such people often believe that bishops should defend a traditional faith and practice, whether or not they actually do so themselves. Many of them were, thus, deeply hostile to the Bishop of Durham.

Strangely, David Jenkins, at the height of the doctrinal controversies that surrounded him, often seemed to share their understanding of the priority of belief. In a long line of radical theologians over the last few decades (Bishop John Robinson was an obvious example and Don Cupitt the most recent one), he appeared to believe that the way to commend Christian faith is to deny those parts of it that now seem to be no longer credible.

Ironically, at the heart of this approach there is a strong missionary zeal. There is a deep concern to interpret the Christian faith in ways that might be accepted by those presently outside the churches. Denying those elements of faith that appear anachronistic is presumably thought to be an important prelude to making Christian faith believable in the modern world. Clear away the accumulated debris first—hack down the wild elders, pull out the nettles, clip out the brambles, and then you can see the garden for what it really is.

Again, I am not particularly convinced by either of these paths. Belief is treated in both as the first step in the Christian life. Further, I doubt if we commend anything by denying those parts that we currently find troublesome. Such an approach always risks the response from the sceptic, 'Well if Christians deny those bits, they are really just secularists like the rest of us'.

That, perhaps, is why David Jenkins has been labelled so often (and so unjustly) as 'the atheist bishop'. Manifestly, a deep faith in God permeates his writings and preaching. At the heart of these is a desire to probe for the mystery of God beyond the conventions of uncritical belief. Yet, his critics often interpret this as simply scepticism.

In any case, are we quite sure that the elders, brambles, and nettles are *not* intended to be a part of the garden? Elder flowers and berries both make splendid home-made wine, and wild brambles have the edge on cultivated blackberries every time. I am not quite so sure about nettles—although some people do swear by nettle tea!

With the varied delights offered in the Christian Scriptures, it is a foolish person who believes that they know what to discard for ever and what to retain. What appears incredible now, may make more sense later. Better to set things that seem incredible to one side for the moment than to discard or deny them. Christian stories may need to be told intact, rather than chopped into bits and then variously labelled as either credible or incredible.

There is an obvious danger here. By placing belonging before belief, I run a risk myself. It might seem that I undervalue belief—regarding it as a matter of peripheral concern. However, nothing could be further from the truth. My point is emphatically *not* that Christian belief should be treated as unimportant. It is, simply, that it is the wrong starting point for mission. Belief needs to be nurtured and shaped by worshipping communities. The priority of mission in Britain at the moment is to foster growth in these communities.

Herein lies the challenge. If belonging is the first stage in the Christian life, then belonging is fast disappearing in Britain today. The area that is disappearing at the most alarming rate is that of child belonging. The situation is now worse than it has been for almost 200 years. Let me explain.

The Sunday school movement in Britain built up steadily throughout the nineteenth century. It was equally strong in the Church of England as it was in the Free Churches combined. By the beginning of the twentieth century, it was only a minority of children that never attended a Sunday school. In wealthy areas, children were sometimes taken to church or joined a church choir instead, but, in working-class areas, strong Sunday schools and weak churches existed alongside each other. A minority of adults attended church (usually in the evening), whereas the vast majority of children attended Sunday school (often in the afternoon and, in some places, in the morning).

Churchgoing and Sunday school attendance patterns were, thus, quite distinct. By the beginning of the twentieth century, adult churchgoing in England was already in considerable decline. The Sunday school movement, in contrast, was at its height. At the high point of adult churchgoing (some time in the 1850s), approximately a third of the population was in church on an average Sunday. Yet, at the high point of Sunday school attendances, at the beginning of the twentieth century, well over half of the child population would have been present on an average Sunday.

Sunday school enrolments, although declining slowly, remained comparatively high until they collapsed in the 1940s or 1950s. By the 1960s they were already reduced to one child in five.

Soon, child attendances at either church *or* Sunday school may be little different from adult attendances at church—a rate of about one in ten. The results can be seen in congregations up and down the country. In the countryside, it is now rare to find a thriving Sunday school or any children in church at all. In towns, Sunday schools may survive, but they are becoming less common. Further, the children who *do* come to church or Sunday school are mostly the children of adults who themselves come to church. In other words, the masses of children in the past who were involved in churches and Sunday schools, but whose parents seldom went to church, are now scarcely involved at all. Church is a place almost entirely for the children of churchgoers.

Another feature that has changed radically is church schools. Before the Second World War, in Britain it was likely that a child would go to a church school. The Victorians spent huge amounts of money building church schools in the belief that Christian instruction should be given to all. Even though a majority of adults probably never did attend church or chapel on a regular basis (except in some isolated rural areas), the Victorians were determined that their children should be shaped by Christian faith. Christian instruction was an essential feature of school education until a generation ago. It was there for all.

The situation is radically different today. The majority of children do not go to a church school. Religious education in school persists and there are even government attempts to strengthen it—supported, according to recent surveys, by a majority of the population. Yet, it is still likely to be quite different from the Christian instruction the Victorians received. World religions feature strongly today and most teachers would hesitate to 'instruct' their children in a Christian faith that they may or may not share themselves.

All of this is very well known. What is less obvious is the profound effect it may have on the possibility of mission. If belonging is usually prior to belief, then most children no longer belong. That is, there is little in the background of most children in Britain today that provides the possibility for Christian belief in the future.

Most children today have no background in Sunday school. No doubt there were weaknesses in the Sunday school system. It seldom made a successful bridge to adult churchgoing—being separate in time and content from church services. Yet, whatever their weaknesses, Sunday schools did give children a framework on which they might construct belief later. Today, they have almost none. Most children do not attend church, do not go to a church school, and have little experience of Christian instruction. In all of these respects they are quite unlike other British children over the last two centuries.

An obvious crack in my argument now appears. I am hinting that, before the rise of the Sunday school movement, the situation was much the same as it is today. Things changed then, so why could they not change again?

This is certainly possible. There are some similarities between the eighteenth century and the late twentieth century. We cannot be too sure of exact churchgoing rates in the eighteenth century, but we do know that many church buildings were in a very poor state of repair. There are also reports that all was not well as far as churchgoing was concerned. It may have flourished in some rural and middle-class areas, but churchgoing may have been thin elsewhere.

So, most children were left uneducated by the churches or by anyone else, yet the situation did change radically in the first half of the nineteenth century. Might this not happen again today?

I will struggle with this question in much of the rest of this book. Yet there is a warning to be made at this stage. The nineteenth century was a time of vibrant growth and increasing optimism. The population doubled in the first half of the century and almost doubled again in the second. The towns were bursting with new life. Trade was expanding throughout the world and the Empire was growing lustily. The idea of progress was widely shared. In this dynamic environment, many denominations flourished. They built heroically—church buildings, huge vicarages, schools and Sunday schools. If you go to South-East Asia today, you will find many of the same features, and you will find many examples of flourishing churches. Yet, in static, depressed Britain today, it is difficult to spot the same vibrancy. The population is no longer growing and people have even been moving house less and less. We are a post-colonial society and are fast ceasing to be a dominant economy. The notion of survival seems to be more apt than that of progress. Conservation as a goal for our society seems to be the best that we might hope for—and even that might be beyond us. It is much more difficult than it was in the last century to see how British churches might flourish in the environment of Britain today.

To make matters worse still, I am suggesting that a framework for Christian belief no longer exists among most young people in Britain today. To rekindle belief among adults, who have had an experience of church or Sunday school somewhere in their background, is one thing. But to initiate belief when there is nothing to rekindle may be quite another. Indeed, to initiate belief when there has been no prior belonging at all seems to be almost beyond credibility.

Whatever else, this surely means that half measures will not do. Churches need courage and vision. If they are to engage in serious mission, then they must be prepared for some bold changes.

CHAPTER 3

Pruning and Planting

Not so long ago, I was asked to speak at a conference in Dublin, preaching in the cathedral there immediately afterwards. What a splendid opportunity.

We arrived in Dublin and were soon admiring its many fine buildings. Then I spotted a sign to St Patrick's Cathedral. Now surely this was where Jonathan Swift was Dean? Having recently reread *Gulliver's Travels*, in a thoroughly unexpurgated version, I had found it quite delicious. Here was this eighteenth-century clergyman poking fun at the foibles of his time, while writing in the guise of a children's fable. It is so spiteful and acid, yet also so endearing. What would most writers give to produce a book like that!

St Patrick's is still a shrine to their most famous Dean. On the north side is a 'Swift Corner', with his mobile, wooden pulpit, his chair, his death mask, his altar-table and a cabinet containing many of his books. The Cathedral even has his snuff box—although no wig or false teeth, as far as I could see. On the south side is a striking bust and the epitaph that he immodestly wrote himself. In translation it reads:

Here is laid the body of Jonathan Swift, Doctor of Divinity, Dean of this Cathedral Church, where fierce indignation can no longer rend the heart. Go, traveller, and imitate if you can, this earnest and dedicated champion of liberty.

How amazing, I thought, that, in a few days time, I would be preaching in Jonathan Swift's cathedral. Just imagine the sermons that his bones must have endured since his death in 1745. Now it was my turn to rattle them.

Then, I discovered that there are . . . er . . . *two* Anglican cathedrals in Dublin. Christ Church Cathedral was to be the venue for my inaugural sermon, not St Patrick's. They made me very welcome there, and I much enjoyed the splendour and the singing. Also, of course, I was untroubled by Swift's bones and they by me. They were a full half mile away. Yet it would have been fun . . .

I found myself pelican-spotting yet again. Not content with two adjacent cathedrals, two massive

43

churches were also built within a candle's throw. So, within the space of a very short procession, there are four Anglican churches competing for congregations in depopulated central Dublin. Not bad for a denomination serving a tiny minority of the Irish population. A veritable flock of pelicans.

There is nothing peculiar in this about Dublin. Flocks of pelicans can be found in most English towns and cities. Disliking the solitary life, they do like to cluster together. I suppose that this is one of the things that I discovered as a curate in Rugby. The two large churches at the centre of Rugby, separated only by the graveyard, were a sort of stone parable. Perhaps they were a hint that all was not well with the churches in Britain.

The story is told in Rugby that it was congregational rivalry that led the Victorians to erect two substantial churches alongside each other. In the early nineteenth century, the parish church was in a bad state of repair, so Gilbert Scott was commissioned to build a replacement. This having been done, some of the congregation at the parish church felt aggrieved. Why should they move into this new monstrosity? So, they decided to commission William Butterfield to build a new body for their original church, albeit retaining the ancient tower (it was to become a model for St Paul's Cathedral in Melbourne—though somewhat smaller, of course, but only somewhat). Hence, the two large churches at the heart of Rugby.

By the late 1960s, the legacy of these heroic efforts was only too apparent. Rugby had pelicans everywhere. Even the little daughter church that I looked after was still equipped for a religious revival. The congregation of 30 were surrounded by seats for

300. Naively, I suggested that some of these seats might be removed. The church council was horrified. 'You never know when they might be needed', was the spoken response. The unspoken response, I suspect, was more biting: 'You never know when we might get a curate who does his job properly and manages to fill them'.

Two years later I went to work in Edinburgh and discovered yet more pelicans. The centre of Edinburgh was awash with pelicans of all descriptions. There was a pelican for every conceivable ecclesiastical taste. There were Presbyterian pelicans galore—some traditional, some modern, some liberal, some Evangelical, one even where Gaelic was spoken. There were Episcopalian pelicans, many struggling with more seats than sitters—some High Church, some very High Church, some very, very High Church, and one or two Evangelical. To add to this, there were also pelicans representing many smaller denominations and sects. Edinburgh positively propagated pelicans.

A decade later in Newcastle, which also had its share of pelicans, I was engaged in full-time research on churches. Working on *The Myth of the Empty Church*, I soon discovered flocks of pelicans up and down the country. They were present in great numbers in almost every rural district, and they were particularly partial to town and city centres. The City of London was a rich breeding sanctuary, and so were cities like York and Exeter. Pelicans adored cathedral towns. Whenever they saw a cathedral, they came flocking from miles around to shelter under its wings. Once congregated there, they nested contentedly together without actually doing anything very much . . . for centuries.

I can strongly recommend the hobby of pelican-spotting. Like most hobbies, you get better at it with time. You begin to notice not just the pelicans that are around at the moment, but even the traces that remain from the past. You are able to explore an ancient town centre, like Winchester, spotting buildings that were once pelicans. Little chapels that now perform other functions—some more obviously pelican-shaped than others. They abound in quite remarkable numbers. Churches have been suffering from pelicanitis for a very long time.

Perhaps I had known this much about country churches from my childhood. My grandfather was a priest on Romney Marsh in Kent for almost 40 years. As children, we frequently used to stay with him and, on a Sunday, I (as the 'religious' one) tended to go on his round of services. Dusty little churches like Snargate and Snave with their evocative smells of damp and musty prayer-books. Even then, in the early 1950s, congregations could be sparse. At times, it was just him and me, saying evensong happily together.

Most folk memories are of large congregations in the past. Perhaps people remember the great occasions, such as harvest festivals, when rural congregations joined together, or perhaps they remember the suburban churches. The truth is that English churches over the last 170 years have never been *simultaneously* full. Even when some churches were crowded twice on a Sunday, there were always plenty of others that were more empty than full. How do I know this?

Victorians left numerous records about the size of their churches and chapels. In part, this was because they financed many churches by renting out their seats to local people. In part, too, it was because they were determined that there should be enough seats in churches and chapels to allow everyone to go to church. Even governments occasionally took an interest in the subject—most notably in the Government-sponsored 1851 Religious Census. As towns grew—some very rapidly indeed—there was a widespread concern that churches and chapels should be made available for all as soon as possible. The moral health of the nation, so it was widely believed, required this.

Many denominations also liked to monitor their relative attendances. There was fierce rivalry between denominations in the nineteenth century and each denomination was anxious not to lose out to another. Rival Methodist chapels, for example, were often built side by side—not motivated by mutual love, but by, sometimes bitter, rivalry. Most Church of England clergymen were obliged to make returns to their bishop, at five- or ten-year intervals, giving numerical details of their own congregations and an assessment of rival congregations. In turn, many other denominations also made private calculations, which were either kept locally or returned to a central administration.

Towards the end of the nineteenth century, newspapers also took an active interest in the relative strength of local congregations. In the 1880s, many printed, in detail, the attendances at every church and chapel for a particular Sunday for the area they served—with or without the permission of the local clergy.

Until fairly recently, it was impossible to compare all of these different records. Some were publicly available, but most were hidden in archives or even in bishops' studies. The individual returns of the unique 1851 Religious Census (which attempted to get ministers of every church and chapel in the country to count their churchgoers) only became available for public inspection within the last generation. Scholars were naturally very limited, then, in what they could discover.

However, now the situation is radically different. County archives and the central collection of records and data make serious comparisons possible. At last, it is possible to compare the information about churches and chapels that the Victorians so assiduously collected, but which sadly they hid from each other. Taking the information about church seats and attendances together, and then relating them to accurate local population figures, produces a quite remarkable picture. This was my task at Newcastle— a task that ranged around the whole of England (and occasionally Wales and Scotland), wherever complete records could be discovered.

The most unexpected finding to emerge from this was that the Victorians drastically overbuilt in many rural and central urban areas. The received wisdom among scholars has usually been that the Victorians never kept pace with the huge growth of towns and cities in the late nineteenth century. As a result, so it was thought, working-class urban communities were often left without adequate provision of churches and chapels. They were, in the process, excluded from church life and, as a result, they rapidly became secular. I reached an opposite conclusion.

The first stage of my analysis was to observe the situation in the countryside. Typically what happened was this. The populations of most English villages grew in the first half of the nineteenth century. There was already a drift to the towns, but this was more than compensated for by a rapid increase in the population as a whole. In the second half of the nineteenth century, the situation changed. Village populations tended to decline very considerably. The drift to the towns had become a stampede. The towns offered employment and freedom. People could earn more money and be independent of farmers and estate owners. They could live their own lives. At least, that is probably what they thought.

The result was that the populations of many villages declined by a third in the second half of the nineteenth century. In some remote areas, the population has continued to decline up until the present day, and, in other areas, it has only started to increase again within the last two or three decades. This huge population shift transformed the country as a whole. A rural population, dependant on farms and estates, became an urban, industrial population. Only in the late twentieth century has it changed again, with service industries now being the largest source of employment in Britain.

What did the churches do in response to these population shifts? Focus their resources on the towns and cities and withdraw rapidly from the villages? Did they follow the people?

Well, no. They undertook one of the busiest rural building programmes for 300 years or more. A staggering number of churches and chapels were built or enlarged in rural areas in the second half of the nineteenth century. In many areas the Free Church denominations competed furiously, raising or borrowing large amounts of money to plant chapels even in the remotest areas. The Church of

England, too, responded energetically. Massive country vicarages were built. Most ancient churches were heavily restored and, typically, an extra aisle was added. Private chapels were built on estates and mission halls at the edges of parishes. All of this while local populations were rapidly declining.

What I had never expected to discover was that, in many rural areas, there was a surfeit of seats. Especially in the remotest areas, by 1901 there were often more seats in churches and more churches (when added together) than there were people in the local populations.

Yet, very few commentators at the time ever noticed this. So obsessed were they with the relative fortunes of their own denominations, that they apparently had no idea that, together, they had over-provided in terms of accommodation. In some areas, for example in rural Yorkshire, there were two seats available locally in churches and chapels for every member of the population. Plenty of choice, no doubt, but not much chance of filling many of the churches.

Soon, I began to discover that a very similar situation had arisen in city centres. Rural populations were shifting to towns, whereas urban populations were shifting to the suburbs. In the City of London, this process began in the eighteenth century. In Liverpool, it began in the nineteenth century. In smaller cities, such as York, this shift was more a feature of the early twentieth century.

Despite depopulation beginning at different times, city centres presented a pattern very similar to rural areas. Denominations continued to build and maintain churches even while their local populations were moving away. Churches were repaired and enlarged and mission halls were added even when city centre populations were shrinking.

The City of London provides a spectacular example of this process. The profusion of Wren churches really did serve a local population there in the early eighteenth century. Church of England churches were also matched by an equal number of Independent chapels. Added together, they could have accommodated slightly less than half of the local population. By the early nineteenth century, however, the population of the City of London had virtually halved, yet most of the churches, and rather fewer of the chapels, were still there. By the early twentieth century, the population was less than a tenth of what it had been 200 years earlier. Only three of the Free Church chapels survived, but most of the Church of England churches were still going strong. Well, not exactly strong: many churches had congregations barely larger than their choirs. Some members of their congregations were travelling in by train from the suburbs to supplement local churchgoers. Yet little more than a tenth of the seats of these churches were now being used on an average Sunday.

Of course, this is a dramatic example. However, there are many other examples from cities and large towns throughout England that, though less pronounced, nevertheless show this pattern. The suburban drift was not met by a national church that responded by shifting congregations out to the suburbs. It tenaciously clung to city centre churches long after local populations had vanished. As will be seen in later chapters, the Church of England is still struggling with many of these churches as it approaches the twenty-first century, and even as it comes to terms with the massive speculative losses and severely reduced returns that the Church Commissioners made in the 1980s.

Another common urban pattern involves the radical change of inner city populations. Again, London provides examples of this writ large. In areas, such as Lambeth, populations drastically changed towards the end of the nineteenth century. In effect, the middle classes moved out to the new suburbs—especially to areas such as Croydon and then Purley—and the working classes took their place. This, too, had a dramatic effect on those churches that had, until then, relied heavily on middle-class churchgoers. So, Lambeth congregations, which generally thrived in the middle of the nineteenth century, were struggling by the early twentieth century. The population had changed, even if it had not actually declined. Those vast Lambeth churches were left stranded in a now largely working-class urban wilderness.

Of what relevance is this to church decline? Obviously overbuilding would produce churches that were more empty than full—in both rural and in central urban areas. However, it need not produce overall decline as high rates of churchgoing in the suburbs might have compensated. So, why did churchgoing decline in England, from about a third of the population in the 1850s, to a bare tenth of the population in the 1990s?

It would be misleading to give a single answer to this question. Ask a number of people and each will give you a different answer—scholars and non-scholars alike. However, one factor is regularly overlooked. Empty churches, in themselves, can foster decline—for a number of reasons.

The first of these has to do with money. The extraordinary overbuilding by the Free Church denominations in the late nineteenth century presented them with massive debts. Many chapels were built speculatively. They were erected with borrowed money in the expectation that they would attract large congregations and then would be able to repay their debts (not too different from the property speculation of the Church Commissioners in the 1980s). In the early part of the century, many new chapels could attract such congregations. Towards the end of the end of the century, though, frequently they failed.

There is abundant evidence of chapels in rural areas, in central urban areas, and even in quite prosperous small towns, that were struggling with debt from the 1880s onwards. Sadly, people who did not even own their homes were sometimes personally responsible for their chapel debts. It is not too surprising, then, that individuals caught in this trap were less than enthusiastic about joining a new chapel when their own chapel had failed.

Linked to this is a second reason for connecting empty churches with church decline. As debt problems mounted, and as congregations became sparser, so chapels and mission halls everywhere began to close. Closure almost always involved a considerable loss of church members.

I measured the congregations of neighbouring chapels in a remote rural area to test out this last proposition. The evidence was startling. In the decade before a chapel was closed, it tended to lose half of its congregation. When it was actually closed, only half of the remaining members of the congregation transferred to neighbouring chapels. And, even in their new chapel, those who did transfer were considerably less active than they had been in their previous chapel. In short, only a remnant from a closing congregation tended to move to, and remain active in, a new congregation.

I say more about this later, but, for the moment, it links to the next reason. One way of avoiding closure is to cluster churches or chapels under a single minister. In most rural areas today, a Church of England vicar will look after three parish churches. In some parts of Lincolnshire, Leicestershire, Hereford, Norfolk and Suffolk, it is many more than this (15, I believe, is the record at the moment). If nothing is changed, the situation will get very much worse in the future. Diminishing revenue from the Church Commissioners will ensure that. Methodists—who have already closed more than half of the chapels that they had in the 1930s—cope with this by having large rural circuits, often staffed by a single minister, albeit assisted by a group of lay preachers.

Unfortunately, clustering churches under a single minister itself tends to foster decline. Even Methodist rural circuits do not escape this decline. Once clergy have charge of more than two congregations, they tend to lose contact and members. Several very convincing surveys have shown this to be the case. Of course, there are exceptions—individual priests or ministers who cope with clusters of churches, while retaining high levels of churchgoing. Yet, in general, the evidence points firmly in the opposite direction. Looking after more than two congregations is, generally, a recipe for a decline in churchgoing.

A fourth reason is slightly more speculative. Empty churches may, in themselves, be offputting, especially for the marginal churchgoer. Sitting in Holy Trinity, Rugby, I was amazed that anyone went to it at all. The fact that Dilwyn Davies could make the congregation of six laugh during his sermon was an extraordinary achievement. I certainly never succeeded. It was the bleakest of environments for churchgoing—however wonderful the individual members of the congregation undoubtedly were. Only the most experienced churchgoer stood a chance of feeling comfortable there. Not surprisingly, then, such churches tend gradually to fade away and close.

One Methodist chapel in the North East had a regular congregation of four. Unfortunately, they were all in their eighties. Their chapel was waiting to die with them. They had failed to integrate any new members for decades and now nothing could change. All was fossilized. How different from a packed mid-Victorian congregation and how different from a charismatic Evangelical congregation in the suburbs today. It is not too difficult to see how the marginal churchgoer can slip into a packed congregation. It is beyond credulity to imagine a marginal churchgoer slipping into a congregation of four octogenarians.

The small congregation fights a constant battle with depression. Because it is small, it often lacks effective lay leadership. Even if it would *like* to start a choir, to run a Sunday school, to have a youth club, to be engaged in care in the community . . . it lacks the human resources to do these things.

By studying churches in a place like Lambeth, this process becomes obvious. In the 1870s, many of the large congregations there undertook an array of youth and social activities. By the 1920s these had largely disappeared. The shrunken congregations could no longer cope. The very activities that might have generated younger members could no longer be supervised.

The final reason is about signals. For the whole of the twentieth century, empty churches have been sending out an unambiguous signal. It is simply this: religion is failing, churches are on the way out, churchgoing is a thing of the past, secularism is the future.

It is frequently supposed that the Great Depression following the First World War was the time when people started to become gloomy about the fate of the churches in Britain. In reality, local newspapers were already making gloomy predictions some two decades earlier. By the early 1900s, they were commenting on the prevalence of the empty church. Pelican-spotting had begun.

Ironically, the first signs of empty churches were not associated with a decline in churchgoing at all. By the 1880s most urban Free Church chapels were already more empty than full—even though, together, they had a larger slice of churchgoers than ever before. They had built so vigorously, that they now had more chapels than they could fill. Yet, what local newspapers typically spotted were chapels that were simply empty. From that, they concluded (prematurely as it happens) that chapelgoing as a whole was declining.

Add these five reasons together and they offer a fairly full account of why empty churches and chapels have tended to foster an overall decline in churchgoing. Without claiming that they have been the *only* reason for this decline, they do go some considerable way to explaining it.

What about suburban churches? Why did they not

flourish instead? Well, actually, they did. There is abundant evidence to suggest that suburban churchgoing remained strong well into the twentieth century. In some suburban areas, it remains relatively strong even today. What tended to happen was that high churchgoing rates progressively moved out of town.

In London, the highest churchgoing rates in the 1850s were in parts of central London and in Hampstead. By the 1880s, central London was declining fast and middle-class Lewisham had become a high churchgoing area. By the 1900s, Lewisham, now distinctly less middle-class, was declining fast and, instead, High Barnet had the highest churchgoing rate. Today, parts of the Medway have relatively high churchgoing rates.

Nevertheless it is hardly surprising that, as low churchgoing habits became established in one area (whether central urban or rural), so people moving from those areas into suburban areas tended to bring nonchurchgoing habits with them. Rural Kent is an obvious example. In my grandfather's day, Romney Marsh was populated by people with Kentish accents. Rates of churchgoing were hardly high even then, but many of the churches did still function. Today, a generalized London accent has saturated the area. The new population seems to have brought with it an even lower churchgoing rate.

Just suppose for the moment that my analysis is correct. Chronic overbuilding in the nineteenth century has bequeathed massive problems to many denominations in the twentieth century. What is the solution? It would appear obvious. We should close all of our underused churches and chapels.

We should be far more pragmatic—as Roman

Catholics in Britain generally have been. With approximately the same number of churchgoers today as the Church of England (or the Free Churches combined), they have barely a quarter of the number of church buildings. They are the only major denomination in Britain to have fewer seats in their churches than their average Sunday congregations. Typically, if one of their churches is full, then they put on another mass at a different time of day. If other denominations have full churches, they immediately start to think about opening additional churches. Catholic churchgoing rates did not start to decline until the 1960s.

So, the answer is quite simple. Close underused churches.

Unfortunately, this, on its own, would almost certainly lead to further decline. Here is the catch-22. Having too many churches seems to foster decline, yet closing churches *also* fosters decline.

Church planting might be a solution to this conundrum. Over the last two decades, the church planting movement has begun to change opinions radically within British churches. It has also had the courage and energy to keep testing different policies. I believe that it should be taken very seriously indeed.

It is still too early to be confident about the overall effects of recent church planting. Local results suggest that a new church, or a new congregation, planted in an appropriate area can generate new churchgoers. Yet, much remains to be tested here. The level of growth, achieved simply by transferring members from one church to another, is only now being properly researched. Equally, few studies of church planting look at churchgoing statistics in a whole population. To achieve growth in one congregation may be exciting. Yet it is distinctly less exciting if this growth is still set in an overall context of churchgoing decline.

Again, a study of church planting over the last 170 years offers some crucial lessons. My own research suggests that the Church of England really did increase its churchgoing rate in urban areas during the first half of the nineteenth century. This growth was strongly connected with a huge burst of energy in some urban dioceses. New schools and new churches were built in many expanding towns. In areas where the population was growing fast, these churches were, typically, crammed to the doors. Urban church planting at this stage was apparently very successful.

It was in the second half of the century that this policy of active building seemed to do as much harm as good. Denominations continued to plant churches and chapels, regardless of whether the local population was growing or not. They also competed among themselves so ferociously that they ignored the overall level of accommodation in any particular area. Yet, what the Victorians observed was that a new church was usually (but not always) full when it was first built. From this they concluded that church planting—as it would be called today—tended to foster growth. What they ignored was that these new churches were often surrounded by older empty churches. Growth in one church was typically associated with decline in neighbouring churches.

The smaller denominations that grew rapidly towards the end of the nineteenth century contributed to this process. The Salvation Army, for example, grew rapidly in many towns and cities in the 1880s and 1890s. Yet, in those towns where they were strongest, the Baptists tended to be much weaker than might have been expected. By the early 1900s the Salvation Army went into very rapid decline—faster than the general Free Church decline. Their rise and fall were both very swift.

My prediction is that this will be the fate of the independent churches or house churches today. They showed very rapid growth in the 1980s. This might or might not continue in the 1990s, but I expect them to collapse very quickly in the early 2000s. Like the Salvation Army a century before, I suspect that they rely too heavily on transfer membership for their growth. They, too, may be tempted to overstretch, establishing a surfeit of separate congregations. To make matters worse, new denominations, and rigorist movements in older denominations, tend to splinter rapidly—producing even more church buildings. All of this could make their decline that much swifter.

Another pattern of church planting, which I will examine in later chapters, involves planting new congregations in existing church buildings. This may offer one of the most interesting paths for the future. Yet if my analysis is correct, then planting more buildings, without pruning back others, would simply add to an existing plethora of buildings with disastrous side-effects.

In the early 1950s, the Church of England planted churches on many new housing estates. Initially, this did seem to generate slight growth in these areas. Sadly, today some of these churches are closed, some are thinly attended, and only some have sizable congregations. There are important questions to be asked later about who exactly paid for such church buildings. Budgeting is crucial for genuine growth.

At the very least, a judicious mixture of planting and pruning seems to be sorely needed. Better still might be to prune *and* to plant without building. Whatever the exact mixture, the status quo can only lead to further decline. The overenthusiastic Victorians have left us with a building problem fostering decline. Without radical planning and action, the problem will remain.

CHAPTER 4

Mission and Membership

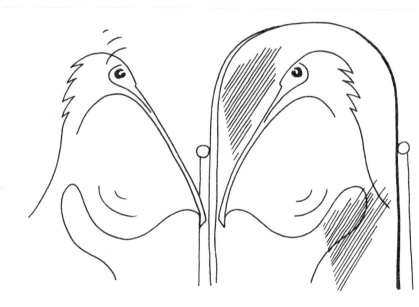

It is time for a game. The rules are simple: take any organization and try to devise a plan to ensure that it fails as soon as possible. You could design a hospital that would be a guaranteed disaster, or it could be a prison, a factory, an office, a school, a university, even a wildlife park for pelicans (filled, of course, with every conceivable pelican predator). I am going to take a youth club.

Probably the most important thing to do is to place the youth club in an area where there are as few young people as possible. It might be a really remote rural area or it might be a well-populated geriatric area. Obviously, it would be a complete disaster, according to the rules, if it was placed in a youthful area. At all costs, that must be avoided. With any luck, there will already be a building available—fully equipped for youth—in one of these rural or geriatric areas.

An added advantage to the geriatric area is that a noisy youth club is certain to antagonize the neighbours. In this respect, it probably has the edge on the deep rural location—unless, of course, it can be arranged that any youth club members are addicted to urban junk food and scatter plenty of litter over the countryside.

The next step is to subsidize the youth club as fully as possible. It is very important, indeed, that nothing is demanded from any young people who actually come to it. If possible, waive any entrance fee. Certainly, accept no money or work in kind for running costs. If possible, give the club a large float for damages. Windows will inevitably be broken, but it is vital that the young people feel no responsibility for this. Best to get someone (perhaps yourself as leader) to repair any windows next morning and without any fuss.

Next, get the youth club to form a clique as quickly as possible. Make sure that it gels so closely that new members always feel excluded. Excellent ways to achieve this are never to advertise, to be secretive about when the club meets, to patronize any potential new members who do turn up, and to keep all jobs in the hands of long-established members. Founder members of youth clubs are particularly adept at doing all of this.

Another good trick is to keep the age profile of the members as old as possible. Preferably, they should be nearing the age when they will be moving on to other things. For example, start a youth club for those just about to go away to university, or time the meetings to clash with revision for A levels.

If possible, make the meetings as routine as possible. Certainly never try to do anything different. Be careful not to challenge the members. A regime of table tennis and CDs is quite a good mixture. Alternatively, make the meetings as embarrassing as possible. It is particularly good to embarrass any potential new members. They must be given the impression as quickly as possible that this is an established club. It is established for existing members only.

Avoid any kind of internal criticism in the club. Members are there to relax. If they get any bright ideas, never listen; it will only bring trouble. The job of the leader is to make things run as smoothly as possible. Sit behind a desk in an office just away from the club. Any signs of trouble and you should be in there. Simply tell them to stop arguing and to go somewhere else if they want things changed. Show them who is boss.

Never accept offers of help. It is the job of the youth leader to run the club. It is thoroughly counterproductive to involve the young people in running their own club in any but the most minor ways. They are either too busy already, or else they will simply make a mess of it. Far better to do almost everything yourself. At least you know that it will be done properly.

That should win. In my own involvement in youth clubs I can remember doing most of these things at some time or another. Try the game yourself—it is not difficult to play—then see whether or not it fits your local church.

If churches are serious about growth, there are things that they can do. In this chapter, I will look at local initiatives—at ways in which individual congregations can seek to grow. In the next chapter, I will take a broader perspective—at how denominations as a whole might plan for effective growth.

The primary motivation for church growth is theological—the conviction that worshipping God in Christ is the most distinctive thing that Christians can do and that this should be fostered in others. The overall mechanism for church growth is structural—denominations that really do have effective strategies for growth. The local means for church growth are congregational—congregations looking for and testing opportunities to grow.

What are these local opportunities for growth? Perhaps the most important precept is simply this: *most people change churchgoing habits when something else is changing in their lives.* If they are not reaching puberty, not getting married, not having children, not moving house, not retiring, or not facing serious illness or bereavement, then people are unlikely to change their practice of churchgoing or nonchurchgoing.

It works both ways. People can resume churchgoing when these changes occur, but they can also lapse from churchgoing. Such changes represent crucial opportunities for congregations, but they also represent potential threats. As so often in life, opportunities and threats tend to travel together.

Most churchgoers are only too well aware of the negative side of change. They can see that young people tend to drift away from active churchgoing as they reach puberty. Once keen members of a Sunday school or of a junior church, they begin to say that church is 'boring'. Or else they show embarrassment at the idea that their friends might discover that they still go to church. Almost every churchgoer who is a parent will be aware of this stage of development.

Another common experience in church life is of someone who is a key figure in a congregation. Perhaps she is a church warden in an Anglican church or a church secretary in a Reformed church. Perhaps he is a treasurer or a verger. Yet, once this person moves house to a new area, he or she may stop going to church altogether. 'Well, I went once or twice to the new church, but it just wasn't the same. It wasn't St Cuthbert's . . . St Runwald's . . . St . . .', is a reason that is given again and again. So, despite appearing to be deeply committed before moving, a strong churchgoer may become a complete nonchurchgoer after moving.

Perhaps the change takes the form of a serious illness or bereavement. Among the most tragic cases that confront any minister are those where a church family cannot come to terms with the serious illness or death of their child. They have heard all the sermons about faith through suffering and they have experienced the ritual from Good Friday to Easter Day many times. Yet they still cannot understand why this has happened to them and to their child. In despair, they curse God and renounce the church, or, less dramatically, their emotions become just too brittle for them to go to church any longer.

The change might be marriage. Many sects know that marriage is a danger point for their faith. If young adults are to continue in the ways of the sect, then it is important that they marry within the faith. Mixed marriages create divisions. The vulnerable world of the sect finds such divisions particularly destructive. They often go to considerable lengths to ensure that growing children mix only with other young people from their sect, so the chances of them marrying anyone not of the sect are reduced as much as possible.

Even some denominations fear divisions created by mixed marriages. It may be no coincidence that British Catholics began to experience a decline in attendances at Mass once mixed marriages started to become the norm. Traditionally, Catholics have criticized mixed marriages because of the effect that they have on children. In truth, they may have an even greater effect on those getting married.

It is one thing for a Catholic couple to continue to practise as Catholics. It may be quite another for a young bride or a young bridegroom in nonCatholic Britain to practise on their own. Before the Second World War, most Catholic marriages in Britain were between two Catholics. Today most are not. This may well be an important factor behind the sharp decline in Mass attendances since the 1960s.

Last, it is not too difficult to see how babies can make life difficult for churchgoers. If the local church is adapted to babies and toddlers, then fine. If it is not, however, life for new parents suddenly becomes traumatic. It can take a brave parent to ignore the scowls of the elderly as their infant tests the famous echo in their empty church. Pelicans are extremely noisy when babies are around. No, too many churches have sound-proof glass galleries, apart of course from the unforgettable one in the film *The Graduate*.

These negative influences are already well known. What may be less apparent is that all of these moments of threat to churchgoing can also be opportunities. If people sometimes lapse from churchgoing at these points (unless congregations are very vigilant), others may actually renew churchgoing at these times. A sensitive congregation will be aware of this and will be watchful—both of those who might lapse and of those who might be encouraged to renew.

Taking the threats in reverse order, it is a truism that the experience of having children for most of us is one of the most profound changes in life. When preparing people for the baptism of a baby, I always use the language of gifts. Most parents are only too well aware that their baby is a gift. They did remarkably little to produce the baby themselves. Yet here is a new life—a life that is going to be their responsibility for the next two decades or more. Alongside feelings of gratitude, are other feelings of vulnerability and responsibility. How can they cope with this new baby? How can they ensure that he or she is going to be a responsible human being?

Naturally, the intensity of these feelings fades, yet this does present congregations with a very real opportunity. Clergy find that they are talking to young people who might for once listen. Yet some churches use this as an occasion to lay down conditions: there can be no baptism unless one of the parents comes to church . . . a few times . . . for three months . . . for a year. The conditions vary from church to church. Not surprisingly, they cause considerable resentment.

More important may be to establish an enduring contact with the new family. Congregations can gradually encourage parents to bring up their child in the context of the church. Doubtless this will not happen overnight. Few clergy report that couples join congregations simply as a result of the baptism service itself—they do need to be nurtured. The traditional Sunday school was the way that this was usually attempted in the past. What many churches lack today is an effective programme seeking to draw new families into their worship, but it is something that most growing churches do have. I am sure that others can learn from this. I will return to this point later in this chapter.

Another major opportunity presented to churches is in the area of serious illness or bereavement. Treated in too clinical a way, there is something horribly crude about talking of 'opportunities' here. There are sects that hover over the sick and vulnerable, offering wonder healings and scavenging for new converts. Quite properly there has been considerable press criticism of such manipulative behaviour.

A sensitive congregation will observe, instead, that it is in moments of serious illness and bereavement that many people first become aware of finitude. It is at these moments that many ask questions about the meaning and purpose of life. Flippancy can turn into a quest for faith.

Congregations could stand alongside people at this crucial point in their lives. Very gently they may be led into a community of belonging, into a community of faith. As noted already, it is most frequently friendships—not verbal conversions—that draw people back to church.

Again, a sensitive congregation will be alert to new people moving into the area. Most of us when we first move to a new place feel vulnerable. Of course, there is the chaos of moving itself. As junk begins to accumulate, moving becomes ever more difficult. Last time we moved we filled a yard with unwanted rubbish; next time it might be the whole garden. However, it is more than that. Moving involves losing friends and disrupting families. It deconstructs comfortable environments and up-ends our daily lives. For this reason, churchgoing habits can also change. A swift welcome and a friendly hand can be very effective for congregations.

Finally, there is youth. Congregations have always known that they should encourage young people, yet all too often they still find this difficult. There does come a point when churchgoing parents must simply remind themselves that, if all goes well, their children will be adults for many years to come. Perhaps they rebelled themselves and still returned to the church. The seeds are planted and one day they will hopefully flourish. Faith can be rekindled.

For the church at large, however, there is surely more to be said. Christian Unions still flourish in many universities, colleges and schools. At present, the more radical Christian organizations, which were strong a generation ago, struggle to survive today. The Student Christian Movement is an obvious example.

With energy and initiative I believe that a variety of Christian organizations could be revitalized among students. It is in the nature of student organizations that they rise and fall and rise again, but what they require are strong-minded individuals who can seize opportunities. Many campus ministries in Britain could be much more effective than they are at present. There are some very important exceptions, but there are also too many that are unconcerned about growth. Perhaps they, also, have become too comfortable.

When a congregation is committed to growth, it becomes sensitive to a whole range of these opportunities. It will develop networks of members around its parish who will be aware of those moving house and those having babies. An important suggestion from the Archbishop of Canterbury is that congregations might even encourage those with newborn babies in their parishes to consider baptism. Rather than waiting for parents to come to them, seeking a baptism, congregations might, rather, do the seeking themselves. They would actively encourage people to come to have their children baptized— as they did in previous centuries.

Such congregations will also be responsive to those facing serious illness and bereavement. Networks of friendship will be used to draw people into Christian worship.

There is nothing very dramatic about any of this. It just requires congregations to be more aware and outgoing. Once they become committed to seeking out new churchgoers, then the rest follows. Soon they will become more attuned to opportunities for growth.

Some large American congregations employ presentable young people to work full-time on recruitment. When someone new appears in the congregation, they quickly establish contact and visit them at home. They go armed with information about what their church has to offer and the opportunities for service that it provides. With so many bright young people looking for work, it should not be too difficult for a congregation in this country to find someone to do the same.

Whenever I discuss growth with congregations, I find that what they fear most is the prospect of door-to-door visiting. Constant visits from Jehovah's Witnesses have undoubtedly shaped their perception of mission. What they fear is that I will tell them that they should be doing *that* themselves. Of course, I never do.

If you have followed my argument this far, you will know how sceptical I am about the idea of converting strangers. Even Jehovah's Witnesses have to visit hundreds of households before they discover a likely convert. In the process, they risk constant abuse and lose almost as many members as they gain. Door-to-door visiting can be a costly business.

Much more effective is for congregation members to use established friendships to encourage others to come to church. Even that encouragement ought not to be made at random. Again, if nothing else is changing in the friend's life, it is unlikely that he or she will respond positively to any amount of 'encouragement'. It is rather like trying to drag someone to see an opera. As an opera lover, I am always conscious of those who have been dragged there and those who have gone because they wanted to be there. At one performance in Edinburgh of *Das Rhiengold*, the half of the audience that had been coerced talked throughout the first five minutes of the overture. They never noticed the silvan music slowly welling up from the orchestra pit. My favourite moment in opera had been ruined. Coerced churchgoing is not much better.

Congregations can become more sensitive to opportunities for growth. They can also attempt to build up new forms of mission designed to promote growth. Worship itself is a vital area of mission. Prayer and study cells are another. A shared ordained ministry is another still. Exciting developments are already beginning to happen in some churches.

As I travel around different churches, I hear frequent criticisms of charismatic congregations. The music is thought to be banal—all those repetitious choruses. The atmosphere is considered to be too emotional—especially the scatterings of Amens and Alleluias. Perhaps it is the actions that offend—people waving their arms around as if they are trees—or it might be the babble of tongues.

Such judgements, though, are highly subjective. I quite enjoy the music and I am even beginning to get used to the arm waving and tongues. It is not everyone's taste, but then neither are Bach, vestments, and incense. Ritual works best if you are on the inside rather than if you are trying to judge it as an observer—your or my ritual is always someone else's superstition.

Even the most verbal sorts of worship still contain rituals.

Some of my Presbyterian students in Edinburgh used to claim that their form of worship was ritual-free. Unlike Anglicans or Catholics, their worship was organized around the Bible. Bible readings, biblical prayers and psalms, and sermons expounding the Bible, entirely shaped their worship. It contained no ritual. When I went, however, I found that their services were highly ritualistic. A nonPresbyterian had to learn how to behave 'decently' in their services—when to stand up, when to sit down, and, especially, when to say Amen (only at the very end of *all* the prayers). The behaviour and speech of the minister was hardly everyday behaviour and speech. Frequently, it was highly stylized. In short, it was the behaviour and speech of well-honed ritual.

Different congregations have many different styles of ritual. It would surely be an impoverished world if everyone had exactly the same rituals. What is important, instead, is that congregations become more sensitive to the styles of ritual that are more accessible to the marginal churchgoer. If congregations are to have at least some of their services designed for them, then there are experiments to be made and tested.

I noted in the last chapter that some growing churches have started to plant new congregations rather than new church buildings. This could be a very important way that many other churches could grow.

Often there is a tension between the needs of long-established worshippers and newcomers. Complaints about trivial choruses and about lack of substance are common from the first group when they react to services actually designed for the second. Equally, it might be unrealistic to expect people who come to church infrequently, at best, to feel comfortable at, say, a sung Eucharist. Better to admit that the content of services is likely to differ according to the stage of development of the worshipper.

Planting a new congregation alongside an established congregation is an obvious way to meet this difficulty. Start an experimental service devised for families who are beginning to feel a need for worship—or at least to feel a need to hand something on to their children. Move all baptisms so they take place during this service. If necessary, ask the central church authorities for a strictly fixed-term subsidy to employ someone to be responsible for this service. It will be his or her job to lead the worship and to recruit from the schools and youth organizations. It will be his or her job to visit parents who might be encouraged to renew churchgoing.

If the experiment succeeds, then it might eventually be incorporated into the rest of that church's life. Members of that congregation could then be encouraged to try more mature forms of worship. If it fails, then drop it and try something else. Local initiatives for growth, such as this one, need to be tested and retested. In this way each congregation might discover its own initiatives that produce real growth.

Linked to this is the role of congregations in providing Christian education. Some people still hope that schools themselves will be able to provide an effective Christian education for young people. It is, as mentioned earlier, the intention of the present Government to strengthen Christian education in schools. Recent Education Acts require a daily assembly of a 'broadly Christian' nature (which, apparently, most parents still want, even if many schools no longer provide it) and the specific study of Christianity, along with two other religious traditions. This does provide a real opportunity for Christians working in schools, and for those clergy who are allowed to speak in schools.

Without belittling this, I do not believe, however,

that it provides a serious substitute for involvement in the worship of a local congregation. In a society that thinks of itself as becoming more and more pluralist—especially regarding religious matters—it would be a mistake to imagine that schools can be agents for encouraging young people to become active Christians. Schools might encourage some young people to take Christianity a little more seriously, but they might also provoke others to be more critical. They might hope that most young people would become more knowledgeable about the relationship of Christianity to other religions, but, from the churches' perspective, none of this really amounts to an effective Christian education. At most it would be a Christian education administered by some more or less sceptical teachers—hardly a very promising environment.

If schools are unlikely to provide effective Christian education today, and separate Sunday schools are rarer than they used to be, then congregations have a vital role in providing such education. Their policy when approaching parents will be to be quite explicit about this. If they wish their children to have any serious Christian education, then it may only be found in the services they provide. Linked to a policy of churches actively canvassing for baptisms would be a further policy of actively recruiting youngsters for Christian education.

There is quite a contrast between Americans and the British on the issue of Christian education. The British have tended to rely on schools to provide this education, supplemented until recently by Sunday schools. Americans have relied, instead, on churches —leaving their schools to be largely secular, as their Constitution requires. As a result, most British children have little or no formal Christian education today. American children, in contrast, continue to go to church for Christian education. It is surely obvious that British children should also be encouraged to do the same.

It is not only children, though, who are in need of Christian education today. Adults, too, are in need. Growing churches tend to have a series of active prayer and study groups as an essential part of their life and development. Some find that, with proper training, these can also be important ways of integrating nonchurchgoers. Once again, through friendships, those who are just beginning to feel a need to worship can sometimes be weaned into a prayer or study group. Part of the success of the house church movement has depended on this. Yet there is nothing about this that cannot be imitated by mainstream denominations.

Finally, there is the ordained ministry. If there is one area in which growing churches are likely to make radical changes, it is surely this. Already there is an explosion of differing patterns of ministry. The congregations in which I have been a nonstipendiary priest have certainly taught me much about resources for ministry that could be exploited further.

One of the most disturbing and challenging discoveries is that stipendiary ministry can sometimes impede the ministry of a congregation. In dwindling congregations, it becomes all too easy to leave everything to the minister.

Because my own ordained ministry has run parallel to a busy academic life, I have been forced to question this. Congregations can easily assume that the nonstipendiary minister will do everything that his stipendiary predecessor used to do. Very early, I discovered that they could learn to think otherwise. I was forced to be clear about the gifts and functions that I might be able to bring to the congregation. In the process, the congregation was asked to supply the missing gifts and functions. Only *together* could we provide all of the gifts and functions normally expected of ordained ministry alone.

Such forms of ministry raise important issues about finance and subsidy. I will explore these issues further in the next chapter. For the moment, though, it is worth observing that, so long as ministry is provided willy nilly to a congregation, it is unlikely to contribute sacrificially. If the finances for a stipendiary minister are directly related to the congregation's finances, then one can be sure that there will be a sense of responsibility.

Of course, it is not simply about finances. Without open-ended subsidies for maintaining ministry, congregations may be forced to look more carefully at their own resources. They may have to provide ministry themselves or, at the very least, a framework for ministry.

Perhaps individuals within a congregation can be challenged to consider training for ministry themselves (ordained or lay). Perhaps congregations can be challenged to make serious ecumenical links in order to provide ministry. Perhaps they can be challenged to finance part-time ministry. With no outside, open-ended subsidies, they will be forced to take these challenges very seriously.

Congregations could, then, cease to be like pelicans in the wilderness. If they did, they might find the Christian life far more engaging. Worship could become distinctly less routine. Prayer and study cells might deepen individual lives. Ministry could be a challenge for the whole congregation, and churchgoers might also feel driven to extend their values more deeply into society at large. That is the theme of the final chapter. Renewed structures for mission is the theme for the next chapter.

CHAPTER 5

Budgeting and Planning

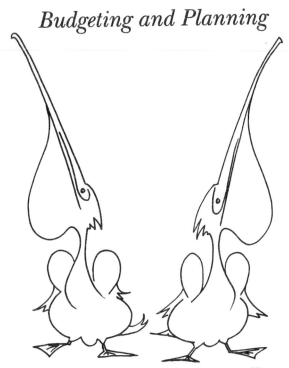

Another chapter, another conference. You might think that my life is dominated by conferences—you are probably right!

This time, it was a request to speak to a meeting of Christian business people in the Midlands. The request came at a particularly busy time, so I procrastinated. For a whole year, I fended off the invitation before agreeing on a date. I was wrong, I should have accepted earlier as it turned out to be one of the most stimulating groups I have talked to recently.

The food was delicious—an array of seafood and salad. A definite improvement on the cold chicken legs that haunt me, as, apparently, they do politicians. I was told that the wine was also delicious, but I had to avoid that. I soon discovered that I needed to stay alert. These were business people who had thought deeply about Christian belonging and wished to be stretched further.

I had prepared to talk about business values. My work at the university at Canterbury is dominated by ethics—indeed, I will return to this theme in the next chapter. Together with the Professor of Philosophy, I run a Centre for Applied Ethics there. Each week, we invite different members of staff to talk about their own area of expertise—hopefully in language that the rest of us can understand. Their brief is simply to highlight ethical dilemmas that arise directly from their work. Sometimes it is a scientist, sometimes a social scientist, occasionally someone from humanities, but some of the most thought-provoking meetings have concerned business and management ethics. So, I decided to talk along these lines to the business people.

As the meal developed, I realized that this was not particularly what they wished to hear. Yes, they did take ethics seriously—they had been trying to do that for years—but what they really wanted to explore was how they might use their business skills as lay people within the churches. Many of them were already church wardens, church elders, or church treasurers, and some were lay readers and preachers. These functions they understood. What they were attempting to discover, though, was how they might use their *professional* skills to help churches that quite obviously lacked these skills.

Pure music. Part of my life on the conference circuit is spent trying to persuade people that business and management skills might have some relevance to the churches. Despite my dog collar, and despite starting with theology, many remain suspicious of this message. 'He is trying to import alien business thinking into the church', is the constant suspicion. 'We don't want the church turned into a business corporation. Leave that to the tele-Evangelists in the United States!'

In one recent survey, senior clergy were given a choice between different ways of seeing their role. Did they see themselves as managers? The answer was a clear 'no'. Functions such as master, builder, and even therapist were preferred. More popular still were traditional terms, such as practical theologian, priest, and preacher. As in many other professions (my own in the university included), management terms are extremely unpopular. Yet here was an audience that actually *wanted* to make links between their professional skills in the business and management worlds and their lay roles in the churches. Even my two persistent critics were absent. There was nobody heckling from the floor, 'What about the Holy Ghost?', or 'Why this concern about bums on seats?'.

Many in this audience already accepted the work of the Holy Spirit and unambiguously wished to see more people attending church. However, as practical business people, they suspected that there were human skills that might pave the way both for the Holy Spirit and for better attendances. These did not conflict in their lives. So, for once, I was able to start further along the argument. I was able to present them with a plan for church growth without having to make too many preliminary justifications. It consisted of the following five steps:

1 *analysis*—identify the points of weakness in the church that foster decline and isolate those that are capable of being changed
2 *planning*—draw up a careful plan based on this analysis, setting out objectives for growth that are capable of being attained
3 *responsibility*—identify ways in which churchgoers may be encouraged to take more responsibility for attaining these objectives for growth
4 *development*—identify opportunities for growth that are not fully realized at present
5 *testing*—having fostered responsibility and implemented development, test and keep testing to make sure that real growth is being attained.

These five steps form a cycle: step 5 leads straight back to step 1 again. There is no let-up as a dynamic organization is never content that all is well. It is always struggling to be better—that is, to achieve more of its real objectives for growth.

Now, obviously, you cannot run a successful business without some such plan; it is simply common sense. Just imagine a business that never analysed itself, never drew up careful plans, failed to make those involved feel responsible, never spotted opportunities, and never tested itself. It would not last very long in a competitive world. But, I am afraid that there are churches that seldom do many of these things.

Perhaps some feel that it is highly unlikely that churchgoers could ever agree on all of these steps. Churchgoers seldom have a common mind. Asked about their objectives and plans, doubtless church people will volunteer myriad points of view. Many, too, will dislike the whole language of opportunities for growth and regard the very idea of rigorous testing in churches as a joke.

This group of business people was scarcely united and they asked searching questions at the end of my talk. However, for once, they were an audience that regarded the idea of a plan for growth—even for the church—as obvious common sense. They did not look on it as Thatcherite ideology, or whatever, but simply as basic common sense. That and nothing more.

Let me assume for the moment that I am still talking to this audience. The five steps should be unpacked before they can be judged adequately. Try to look at them as more to do with common sense than high ideology—simply as practical steps that prudent denominations might take if they wish to grow.

The first step demands analysis. I have already attempted to provide this in the previous chapters. However, what I have yet to do is to identify those points of structural weakness in British churches today that are capable of being changed. Analysis should also point up areas of strength that can be related to opportunities in step 4.

In terms of a plan for growth, it is no use spending too long on points that are impervious to change. For example, there is little purpose hoping that Britain will spontaneously stop being apathetic and static. That appears to be the given context for the

British church at the moment. Instead, denominations might identify points of weakness in their own ways of working that are capable of being improved.

There is one point of weakness that particularly fits this description. It might be summarized by a single word . . . subsidy. If my analysis in the earlier chapters is correct, then many British denominations— and especially the Church of England—have been suffering for many years from the effects of unchallenged, open-ended subsidy. To put it bluntly, they have subsidized their own long-term decline.

In the nineteenth century, several denominations built churches and chapels beyond their capacity to fill them. Then some (particularly the Church of England) continued to subsidize these churches, even when effective local populations disappeared. Through economic subsidies, of one sort or another, they maintained empty churches that themselves contributed directly to a decline in churchgoing.

This process can be illustrated by a boom town of the mid nineteenth century, Barrow-in-Furness. Accurate churchgoing and church building records have been kept in this area since the 1820s. This shipbuilding town grew from nothing between the 1850s and the 1880s. It provides a remarkably complete example of a process that took place on a larger scale in many other parts of Britain. It also shows how different denominations financed their building activities.

In the 1820s, the whole parish of Dalton-on-Furness was a rural, Anglican enclave. With a population of just over 2000, it had 3 Anglican churches and just 1, tiny Methodist chapel. About a third of the population went to church regularly. By the early 1850s, the population had doubled, churches had expanded slightly, but the churchgoing rate was little changed. It also remained predominantly Anglican.

Then, like some American boom town, Barrow-in-Furness, as it became known, suddenly exploded within the parish and reached a population of almost 50 000 by the 1880s. Interestingly, the churchgoing rate remained at about a third of the population, yet its composition changed radically—for every Anglican churchgoer, there were now three Free Church chapelgoers.

Methodists built prodigiously in this new town. Each of the main Methodist denominations had a cluster of rival chapels. Baptists, Congregationalists, and several other smaller denominations also joined in. Not to be outdone, the Anglicans decided to counter this Free Church 'invasion' by opening four, identical, large churches on the same day—each dedicated, naturally enough, to an Evangelist.

Unfortunately, the Anglican building programme had been delayed too long. The dramatic population growth of Barrow-in-Furness slowed down. Within three years of being built, three of the four Anglican churches were more empty than full. Two decades later, most of the clergy were making gloomy reports to their bishop. All but two in the town reported that attendances at Communion were 'unsatisfactory'.

How did the different denominations finance this extraordinary building activity? The Anglican programme is exceptionally well documented. At a cost of £6000 for each church, the Duke of Devonshire gave half the money and the Duke of Buccleugh, the shareholders in Furness Railway, and Barrow Steelworks provided most of the rest. Only a sixteenth of the total cost of the four churches was raised directly from local churchgoers. In contrast, most of the money for chapel building appears to have been raised by local chapelgoers

It was extremely difficult for the Free Churches to compete with the enormous subsidy that the Church of England received in the nineteenth century. In the countryside, Anglicans could rely on rich patrons and on tithes exacted from farm land. As a result, they could build churches and maintain incumbents even in the remotest, most depopulated areas. In the second half of the nineteenth century, it was quite common to find a full-time vicar set in a parish of fewer than 200 people. Typically, he would still have a large vicarage and a well-repaired church.

Subsidy made this possible. It also made it extremely difficult for the Free Churches to compete, yet compete they still did. Even when they manifestly could not afford to compete, they still competed. Subsidy also allowed Anglicans to maintain city centre parishes long after local populations had disappeared to the suburbs. What is more depressing, it still allows Anglicans to do such things today.

The City of London is, again, instructive. Three hundred years after its population started to decline, the Church of England is still struggling to make sense of the City's Wren churches. There have been three major inquiries in the twentieth century attempting to resolve the issue. There is still considerable and powerful pressure to maintain these churches, despite the fact that most of them effectively ceased to function as parish churches at least a century and a half ago.

Throughout the twentieth century, the Diocese of London has been trying to make sense of the simple fact that, however beautiful, most of these churches have no obvious function. Most act as a continuous drain on historical resources. Any other denomination would have been unable to delay for so long. Only the Church of England has had the inherited wealth to allow it to do so. Sadly, this wealth may have done it more harm than good.

Any plan for growth faced with this evidence might conclude that the Church of England (and perhaps other denominations as well) lacks any serious policy on subsidy. American churches, in contrast, still compete vigorously, but they tend to be much more rigorous about subsidy. Of course, American churches do not have all of the answers about church growth. Over the last two decades, many mainstream denominations there have experienced considerable decline (usually to the advantage of more conservative denominations and sects). Yet, taken over the course of the twentieth century, American denominations as a whole have increased or maintained high churchgoing rates, while Anglican and Free Church congregations in Britain have declined almost without interruption.

Subsidy needs to be given a time limit, it needs to be controlled, and its effectiveness needs to be tested again and again. If an American congregation is subsidized, it is typically told how long this subsidy will last. At the end of that period it must sink or swim, unless it can really justify further subsidy. Congregations compete for subsidy and, in turn, must expect their use of subsidy to be checked and tested.

If I had a single motto to offer British denominations it would simply be this: *subsidize mission not maintenance.* Common sense suggests that subsidizing maintenance stifles local initiative. Providing congregations with churches financed by outside money, and giving them a full-time minister, whether they pay for this eventually or not, are both recipes for inaction. With the radically depleted resources of the Church Commissioners, the Church of England may now have to manage without them— and perhaps it might be healthier if it did.

There are, of course, several different ways to reduce dependence on subsidy. The most obvious is to require all established congregations to be self-sufficient. Many fear that this will simply produce a congregational church. I am not sure that this is really the case elsewhere in the Anglican Communion or even within all of the Free Churches here in Britain. The Church of Scotland, even as a national church, tends to have congregations that are much more self-contained financially.

Nevertheless, there is a strong case for arguing that small clusters of churches should hold a common budget. Provided that these clusters are, indeed, small (present-day Anglican deanery synods, for example, are usually too large for this purpose), I believe that this could promote greater responsibility. The immediate effect might be to ensure that congregations in suburban areas do not have a monopoly of resources. By linking them with congregations in more deprived areas, a wise policy would ensure that they felt mutually responsible.

The second step in my list involves careful and continuous planning. Those who work in other organizations will know that written plans are increasingly becoming the norm. In the university world, for example, it is no longer acceptable to be vague about aims and objectives. Universities require us all to plan and to review our plans at regular intervals; questions are asked. What are the priorities for research in your area? How many students do you plan to attract? How can you realistically achieve this? What new initiatives might be started? What is the role of present and future staff? And so forth.

Of course, some university dons deeply despise all of this. 'How can you measure real scholarship?', they ask. They believe that their role is simply to be there as 'real scholars', regardless of how many students wish to study under them or how many books they produce themselves. Yet, most of us are beginning to see that such attitudes can be extraordinarily arrogant. They assume that only university staff know what they should be doing. They do not have to listen to students and they do not have to convince the taxpayer. In reality, no university today thinks it can still function on this basis. Student numbers and identifiable research do matter.

In most churches, however—with a few important exceptions—similar issues are often left vague. There is something almost indecent about asking questions about objectives. Most other professions and organizations find them indispensable if they are to operate effectively. Perhaps churches, too, should be expected to plan for greater effectiveness. There is no particular virtue in being ineffective.

If the logic of previous chapters is accepted, then growth should become a major objective of churches. Of course, numerical growth is not everything. Overall growth may even be exceedingly difficult. Granted this, it is still important. In a context of a long-term decline in churchgoing, it should now become a priority. Planning should, I believe, include growth as an essential element.

People in business studies often resort to theological language at this point. No doubt as a result of American influence, there has been much talk about 'mission statements'. Even otherwise secular British academics suddenly start to talk about mission. A forceful word like mission—implying a policy of objectives that are taken very seriously—seems to be required in business. Most recently, there has been a tendency to talk about 'vision' instead—although even vision has theological connotations. Perhaps it is time that a theological term, borrowed by the secular world, should be returned to the churches, but retaining some of its new force. There is a rich irony involved in all of this.

If churches really do plan for growth—even producing mission statements committing it to a plan for growth—then the next three steps in my list follow on naturally. They will be concerned to foster a sense of responsibility or 'ownership' among congregations. They will be concerned to look for realistic opportunities for growth. They will also be determined to test and retest their procedures carefully to see whether or not they have produced genuine growth.

Ownership first. This term suggests that an organization is most effective if it carries those working in it along with its central aims. A more paternalistic view was that management decides something and then requires workers to conform. The workers were then either bribed or penalized in order to produce conformity. In contrast, the modern concept of ownership suggests that all members of an organization have a real role in decision making and feel responsible for the decisions once made.

Managing a budget is one of the most important ways of ensuring this sense of ownership. In many churches, and particularly in the Church of England, there is a separation between money raised and money received. Not surprisingly, it is difficult to convince congregations to give realistically. If an ordained ministry is provided for a congregation, regardless of how much that congregation actually contributes to central resources, then members are unlikely to give sacrificially. Only when congregations know that the form of ministry they have is directly dependent on their own contributions will they 'own' the process.

A consequence of ownership in this sense is that congregations must also be responsible for their own ministry appointments. Compare the way a typical Anglican vicar was until very recently appointed in England with that of his or her counterpart in the United States today. Here, a single candidate was suggested by the bishop, usually without the post being advertised. There, a selection committee is set up by a congregation and the position advertised. Here, the person suggested would visit the parish, having discreet talks with key individuals. There, the selection committee draws up a short-list and interviews candidates. Here, an agreement was reached between the bishop and the church council. If this failed, the bishop might offer the parish another candidate immediately or advise the parish that they might have to wait some time for another candidate (if they were still foolish enough to turn down the original candidate). There, the selection committee draws up a provisional contract with the successful candidate. Here, the agreed candidate was, and usually still is, appointed with a full freehold. There, the successful candidate is given an initial contract to be reviewed after a specified time. Here, the parish had, and usually still has, their new vicar for as long as he wishes to stay. There, the parish has their new vicar for as long as he or she fulfils a specified role to his or her own satisfaction and to that of the parish.

Quite a contrast. Although some English dioceses are certainly changing, many might still find the American system threatening. I suspect that it is actually more healthy. It keeps a dynamic relationship between clergy and congregation, and it rewards energetic, dynamic clergy. Whatever system is used—there are several available—a dynamic denomination that is committed to growth should be prepared to encourage and reward (perhaps even financially) those clergy who are most effective in promoting its objectives. Growth as an objective does need to be recognized in some tangible way.

One objection that I constantly meet is that such a policy would, in effect, denude the countryside, as well as city centre and urban deprived areas, of clergy. Only the suburbs would be able to afford to have clergy.

Frankly, I am not convinced about this—not least because of the 20 years when I had responsibility for churches while working as a full-time academic. I *know* that a full-time, paid ministry is not the *only* effective form of ministry available to churches, there are many others: non-stipendiary ministry, part-time ministry, post-retirement ministry, ecumenical ministry, trained lay ministry. It is not so much that alternatives do not exist, but, rather, that they will seldom be taken very seriously so long as subsidies are provided to maintain an ever more stretched stipendiary ministry.

We are back to the question of subsidy once more. Only a denomination that relies so heavily on subsidy would imagine that it is prudent to subsidize rural incumbents to look after ever more and more parishes—despite the contribution that this policy makes to decline. Only such a denomination would pay for rural and central urban incumbents when local populations have largely disappeared.

In contrast, congregations—or small clusters of congregations—that are responsible for their own budgets and for their own appointments could act differently. It would be for them to decide on the form of ministry that best suits their needs and which they can afford. They might decide to train people for non-stipendiary ordained ministry, for fully trained lay ministry, or for ecumenical ministry. That would be for them to decide. How many church buildings they need and can afford would, again, be for them to decide. It makes little sense for central Anglican or Free Church authorities to try to impose such decisions on local congregations. That hardly promotes ownership.

In turn, this would liberate central church authorities to focus, instead, on strategies for growth. With the newly available historical resources, they would be free to develop fresh initiatives responding to opportunities for growth.

Here is the greatest challenge. What opportunities for growth are there in apathetic, static Britain today? Given the will and sufficient resources, what really could be done to halt decline and to promote growth? The various suggestions made in the last chapter were related to initiatives by local congregations. At a denominational level, it should be possible to direct and finance some of the most able and energetic clergy and trained lay people to engage in growth projects. These might be at Sunday school or junior church level. They might be with young adults. They might involve planting new congregations for families currently outside formal church structures. Resources could be freed for this work, providing subsidies on a strategic, but limited term, basis.

Finally, such initiatives should be tested at regular intervals. One of the ironies of appraisal—the most widely known form of testing among professional groups—is that, at first, individuals often resist it strongly, but many actually enjoy appraisal when it happens. In many professions—and increasingly among clergy as well—testing in the form of appraisal is becoming an accepted procedure. Testing in the form of audit is usually regarded as more threatening. Perhaps I should explain the difference.

Appraisal typically takes the form of people putting on paper what they have been doing over the previous year and what they intend to do over the next. Of course, each job is distinctive, so appraisal forms for each profession will be constructed differently. In the academic world, the three headings under which dons are asked to analyse their roles are research, teaching, and administration. Typically, the individual will then be required to discuss this form with a senior colleague, knowing that it will be produced in appraisal again next year. By that time, it will be known to what extent intentions from the previous year have been put into action.

It is actually quite satisfying for many of us to

review our work in this way. There is a sense of achievement at being able to say that we have accomplished at least some of the things that we said we wanted to achieve at the start of that year. Admitting failure is also important. Perhaps we were overambitious, or perhaps we just ignored roles that are still important and must now be taken up. Either way, there is a sense of direction and planning built into appraisal. A job should no longer feel as if it is just one darned thing after another!

Audit usually requires more careful measurement, as well as assessment, by those we are attempting to serve. At some of the more efficient clergy conferences I speak at, I find that I am subjected to an audit. Afterwards, someone will write to me, telling me the sort of comments made on assessment forms by the clergy at the end of the conference. Again, this can be reassuring. It can also suggest points for improvement.

Doubtless, at the conference itself, some people had already informed me that I was talking rubbish, but, from the audit, I learn of other shortcomings: my delivery was inaudible, my jokes were distracting, my visual aids (usually nonexistent) were less than professional. I am not expected to change all of my ways in the light of every criticism, but I am wise if I take the criticisms seriously.

When I first encountered a student audit (some 15 years ago now), undoubtedly I felt threatened. Why should students tell *me* how to teach? I thought that *they* were the ones who were coming to learn. With a bit more experience, and, perhaps, a little more humility, I have learned otherwise. Students are not always accurate, but they are able to do something that I cannot do myself—observe from the outside what I am trying to do. If more objective criteria are also added to this, such as how many students enrol for my classes and what grades they achieve, then I am given valuable information about the quality of my teaching. The students, in turn, may be encouraged to discover the amount of audit built into the ever more elaborate system of examination marking today.

Another form of audit that industrious academics have always faced is book reviews. Even as I write, I can feel the hot breath of the reviewer of this book! When I wrote my first book, I can well remember anxiously invading the periodicals section of the library. Had anyone reviewed my book? At the time I had not met anyone, apart from my students, who had actually read it. If it had been reviewed, what was the verdict? Anxious stuff. Some hurt authors immediately leap into print when they encounter the mildest criticism of their newborn baby. Having splattered the dirt myself as a youthful reviewer, I soon realized that it would be ridiculous for me to do that.

Perhaps audit should be applied more rigorously to churches, too. Clearly the Assets Committee of the Church Commissioners has, until very recently, lacked an adequate system of audit. Their investment policy, which proved so expensive for the Church of England in the 1980s, was not subjected to the sort of risk analysis required in other organizations dependent on investment income. The results have been obvious.

Some clergy do have the courage to give assessment forms to their congregations. How effective are the sermons? Could the intercessions be improved? How do congregations think the clergy should apportion their time? These and many other questions.

If they are serious about growth, then audit is needed for *all* congregations. What initiatives are being attempted to generate growth? How effective are they? Are new members of the congregation coming from other churches or from outside church structures? What attracted them to a particular church? What else might be done? How time effective are the things that are already being done?

I do know of congregations already doing this kind of audit and perhaps all congregations should do it on a regular basis. The more serious they are about growth, the more prepared will they be to listen to the assessment of informed outsiders. Churches really could learn from each other. There are strategies that can be copied directly and others that need to be adapted to meet local situations. Only rigorous testing can tell the difference.

If long-term decline is to be reversed, it will require a long-term set of strategies to achieve this. However much we rely on the Holy Spirit, we are still required to use our gifts and resources as effectively as possible. Careful and continuous planning is essential. A serious plan for growth is long overdue in many denominations.

Well, that is the gist of what I said to these Christian business people and how splendid it was to discuss plans for growth with people who appreciated the virtues of planning.

CHAPTER 6

Values and Care

When I travel around the Anglican Church, I am frequently shown social action undertaken by local Christians. In Hong Kong and Australia, particularly, I saw some remarkable projects.

One of the most impressive projects was run by a young man in Australia who would surely have been a millionaire in the mainstream business world. He had very considerable entrepreneurial skills.

Working through his local congregation, he set up a series of work ventures in the city. One of these had formed a small cooperative factory mending and renovating computers. He had noticed that, in many big businesses, faulty, or even just dirty, computers are simply discarded. So, he organized a group of unemployed people with the necessary skills and set up this very successful cooperative, mending and then selling computers back to the big businesses.

Another project was concerned with work training, especially in basic secretarial uses of computers. From charitable and local authority sources, he had raised the money needed to rent premises and to acquire the necessary hardware. The long-term unemployed were then encouraged to come to the project in order to acquire new skills that might make them employable.

The third project was the most impressive. He had rented a downtown office block and was filling it with a whole series of business initiatives. Those wishing to start a small business could rent a little office space at an affordable price within the block. They were then offered free professional advice by those working for the project on how they might best run their business. An amazing spectrum of individuals and groups had begun to occupy the block.

His motivation for doing all of this was clear. For him, it sprang directly from his life within a Christian community. Having seen the projects during the week, I was invited to preach on Sunday at his church on their connection with the Gospel. The link was clear: *our values are moulded by the communities we belong to.*

We live in a culture that seems to have temporarily forgotten this link. Once it might have been obvious that the values we hold owe a great deal to the communities we belong to. The Victorians certainly assumed this. A strong concern about morality, as noted earlier, was one of the reasons they spent so much time measuring the size of their churches and the number of churchgoers. In 1851, as we saw, even the Government became involved in this task. The assumption behind it was often quite simple—namely, public morality will suffer if the churches collapse.

Today, we have become sceptical about this assumption. Our liberal culture assumes, instead, that people must make up their own minds afresh about what is right and what is wrong. Individuals must agonize about this on their own. There is little that society, even through the churches, can say on such matters. Values are a matter of personal choice. Society can extend choice and protect choices, but it should not itself prescribe values.

How then do individuals decide on values? Opinions differ on this. Some believe that values consist solely of emotions and feelings. If I say that something is good, I am really saying that it feels good to *me*. Conversely, if I say that something is bad, I am saying just that *I* find it distasteful. What is good is what feels right for me—it might, of course, be bad for someone else. Thus, what I consider to be bad does not feel right for me, and that, too, might be the reverse for another person. All issues of good and bad are relative according to this thinking.

Others argue that this is unsatisfactory. They insist, instead, that there must be logical reasons for deciding on the difference between good and bad. It

101

would be intolerable if we came to the conclusion that, say, the Nazi death camps were simply matters that we happen to find in poor taste. There must be reasons for believing that these death camps were actually wrong. Just imagine a world in which they were regarded as acceptable. Would that be a rational world?

I do not want to deny the roles of either feelings or reason in moral action. If we had no feelings, I doubt if we would ever act in moral ways. Further, if we can give no reasons at all for acting morally, then we risk all kinds of irrational demands. Both are important in morality. Yet, I do not believe that they are sufficient. They both tend to underestimate a more obvious source of moral values—namely, the communities to which we belong.

I am convinced that we should take the role of moral communities more seriously in Britain today. Enduring values do not simply grow on trees, in the wilderness, or wherever. They are not simply plucked from the ether or invented by each and every individual afresh. Values that endure are taught and handed down within communities. However dimly individuals perceive the values that their communities carry, these values endure. They do not depend on the whims or particular logic of individuals.

Recently, I have been studying the behaviour of people who act beyond what might be termed self-regarding interest. Self-regard is obviously important. Indeed, it is tragic if individuals lose self-regard altogether. In urban wildernesses, there are, sadly, many who have. Yet, for most of us, self-regard comes as naturally as breathing. Our problem is to understand why anyone should act *beyond* self-regarding interest. Why *is* the behaviour of some people altruistic?

There are cynics who deny that anyone acts beyond their own self-interest, and claim that *every* human act can be reduced to self-interest without too much difficulty. Take, for example, those who care for a spouse with Alzheimer's disease. It is quite possible to explain their behaviour in terms of self-interest. Perhaps they just enjoy caring for someone who is so helpless. They get a deep sense of satisfaction from caring. Or they reason to themselves that caring in this way is basically prudent, that if and when they are helpless themselves, they wish someone to care similarly for them. Or perhaps they believe that there is some future reward for caring for their spouse—even a reward in heaven.

All of these explanations might seem fairly plausible, but I am not sure that any of them really fits the facts.

Since I first started to write about carers of people with Alzheimer's disease, I have had several very moving letters from people deeply involved. It can be a thankless business. Sufferers can be confused and exceedingly difficult for many years. One sufferer explained how it felt in the early stages of the disease: 'My whole brain is like a dark thunderstorm'. Tragically, the disease can affect some in early middle age, thoroughly distorting their personalities. Mild and gentle people can become bitter and complaining instead. It is not a disease that easily equates with warm glows for carers—it can cause deep distress for carers and sufferers alike.

Most carers, when asked why they continue to care

for difficult spouses or relatives, talk not about 'satisfaction' but about 'duty'. They feel that they ought to do this, quite regardless of any personal reward. The level of care that they give exceeds any prudential considerations about care that they might one day receive in return. Indeed, if simple prudence was their primary motive, then there are many more manipulative ways of achieving this. It is not too difficult for the manipulative to play on the emotions of the naive. Even heavenly rewards tend to be mentioned, at most, as an afterthought by carers. A sense of duty usually comes first.

This, I believe, is very important. We assume so often that we live in a self-regarding society that we tend to overlook such daily acts of altruism. Even churches tend to celebrate heroic acts of saintly altruism in the past and forget about the selfless action of many of their own elderly very much in the present.

There are many other examples of daily altruism that we could also celebrate. Another area that I have been examining recently is the behaviour of those who have AIDS. There is growing evidence to suggest that altruism is abundant in this area too.

Experienced doctors tell me that most of those with AIDS are only too keen to ensure that their terrible infection is not passed on to other people. The idea of 'revenge sex' belongs more to tabloid newspapers than to anything else. Whatever their behaviour in the past, most of those with AIDS, or who are HIV positive, are deeply concerned about the health of others.

Then there is the behaviour of the many people who still do voluntary work in Britain today. Again,

we sometimes talk as if voluntary work has disappeared—as if it has all been handed over entirely
to professional welfare agencies.

The reality is quite different here as well. Charity
shops, meals on wheels, hospital visiting, prison
visiting, scouts and guides, and many other religious
and secular organizations depend on voluntary
work. So does the simple act of people being good
neighbours.

Why do people do all of these things? Typically, we
try to answer this question in terms of inner motivation (as I have just done). But another way of
answering it is to look at the social or community
structures that support altruism. Are there links to
be made here?

A series of fascinating surveys has strongly suggested that there are. Most scholars have overlooked
them. As I mentioned in Chapter 1, these surveys
suggest that religious factors are far more important
than is usually realized. Religious factors may even
be more important than most carers themselves
realize.

The strongest finding suggests that the person who
is most likely to be involved in voluntary work, of
one kind or another, is both a believer and a churchgoer. Whereas the person who is least likely to be
involved in such work is both an unbeliever and a
nonchurchgoer. Religious differences are actually
more important for once than differences of social
class, age, or sex.

This is such an unexpected finding that it requires
some unpacking. Of course, everyone can think of
someone who is a declared atheist and (not un-
naturally) never goes to church, yet who is deeply

involved in voluntary work. We can also all think of members of every congregation who would be most unlikely to lift a finger to help anyone, no matter how deserving. There are always exceptions, but that is not the point. Rather, it is that the believing churchgoer is some three times more likely than the unbelieving nonchurchgoer to act in an altruistic way.

Even if those forms of voluntary work that are directly related to churches are removed from the analysis (and I do not really see why they should be removed), the general prediction still holds. Believing churchgoers are the people most likely to be involved in voluntary work, regardless of whether this work appears to be churchy or secular.

One factor that tends to mislead people is the 'secular' front of many caring agencies. There is a process here by which this front is created. An organization, like The Samaritans or Relate (formerly the Marriage Guidance Council), begins as a project initiated mainly by Christians. The organization soon decides that it should be open to all—Christians and nonChristians alike—so, its Christian roots are played down. Finally, it appears as if it is a purely secular organization.

In a sense, it might well be, yet the evidence suggests that there is still an unexpectedly large proportion of Christians actively working in such organizations. Because volunteers are also guided by the secular ethos of the organization, they seldom discuss their church connections. Therefore, they, too, may be unaware of the full extent of Christian involvement in their organization. Even in the remarkable work venture projects that I saw in my travels, Christian involvement was often less than explicit. Sometimes this was because of the very success of the projects. Their training was so effective that they subsequently employed some of those trained, regardless of whether or not they were Christian. At other times, it was simply because they wished to be inclusive; they saw their role as more to do with Christian caring than with explicit Christian preaching.

This may account for the gap in our perception of voluntary work. But it does not quite explain the link between churchgoing and care in the community? The causal connection might work either way. It could be that the sort of person who is involved in voluntary care is also the sort of person who would, typically, go to church. So, it is the fact that the person has a caring personality that connects care and churchgoing. Alternatively, it could be the churchgoing itself that stimulates people to care.

It is always difficult to be certain of the exact nature of such causal links. Yet the survey evidence does seem to suggest that it is churchgoing that is mostly the *cause* and that voluntary care is mainly the *effect* of this. In addition, when asked why they started to go to church in the first place, few people suggest that it was because of their role in voluntary care.

There is another link that takes me back to the first chapter. Going to church involves belonging to a worshipping community. As I have stressed several times already, in a society that seldom worships, worship is, today, the most distinctive thing that Christians do. In worship, we may glimpse the deepest levels of reality. We are pulled beyond ourselves and invited to put God and our neighbour before anything else. A stress on goodness beyond self-regarding interest permeates Christian worship. It may not be too surprising, then, that this precept tends to filter into the everyday lives of Christians.

A mistake that is sometimes made is to imagine that this implies that congregations will be perfect. Sometimes we talk as if our new life in Christ is a fulfilled reality. On this understanding, it is the role of the Christian community to be an example to the world at large. Watch us and you will be able to see how Christ intends human beings to behave. We are already perfected in Christ. Yet, we know perfectly well that this is not the case. Just when we attempt to set ourselves up as an example to others, our bad temper or bad behaviour betrays us. There is no shortage of critics ready to point this out. Tabloid newspapers, for example, just love stories about 'randy reverends'.

Often, I go to sung evensong on a weekday at Canterbury Cathedral. Driving to the Cathedral is now almost impossible, even if I had a place there where I could park. So I walk instead. The street leading to the Cathedral is strewn with beggars, old and young, some sober but most fairly drunk. Wearing a dog collar, I never know how to react. I know that they will instantly call out to me for money, and I have no idea how I should respond. When I offer food, they seldom seem very pleased. Money is what they want, doubtless to get even more drunk. To keep my guilt flowing, they shout rich abuses after me as I go down the street to evensong. 'Is that your idea of a xxxxxxx Christian!'

Of course we are meant to be an example—a light

shining in a bleak world. If we are honest, though, we are only too aware that we are *not* always good examples. So, Christians are not immune to marriages breaking up. It is a growing problem among Anglican and Free Church clergy in many parts of the world. Catholic priests also have their problems. Alcoholism and sexual promiscuity seem to be recurrent failings.

Notoriously, we Christians squabble among ourselves and sometimes we regard each other as the real enemy. Wars between Christians have disfigured the world for most of our history. Christians have done appalling things to other Christians and to nonChristians alike. It would take a brave person to claim Christian history as evidence of the moral probity of Christians.

Perhaps Christians are more bearers than exemplars of values. In worship, especially, we are confronted with values that we are challenged to make our own. These values may spill over into society at large, blurring still further any moral distinctions between Christians and nonChristians. Values saturate our readings from the Bible, our prayers, our hymns, and our liturgies. At every point, we are challenged to move beyond self-regarding interest. We are challenged to see the world as a gift from a God who loves us and requires our love in response.

It is in worship that we find the common link between mission and care.

Some believe that care is a form of mission. It is the role of the church to be deeply involved in care within the community. Through this care, others will be able to see something of the attractiveness of

Christianity. The sight of caring Christians will encourage others to become Christians themselves. Other forms of mission are either unnecessary or misguided.

A number of Victorian churches worked on this principle. In York, for example, one of the late Victorian churches was deeply committed to mission through care. The local vicar reported to his bishop that, every week, his church gave away many sacks of coal, as well as food and clothing, to the poor. Few of the poor actually came to church, he admitted, but gradually they would see the truth of the Gospel in action.

Much of the work of the Salvation Army has been strongly committed to mission through care. It has also been a major justification of recent Anglican work arising from *Faith in the City* (Church House Publishing 1985). There is a long and impressive record of care by churches over the last hundred years. It is, I believe, an essential part of the Gospel. However, I am not so sure that it has very much to do with mission.

Observing the churches engaged in this action were those two astute observers of urban poverty, Charles Booth in London and Seebohm Rowntree in York. Both pious Quakers, they were also strongly committed to the relief of poverty. Much of their work is still studied and quoted at great length by urban social scientists. However, their detailed and documented studies of local churches in London and York at the turn of the century are mentioned far less. For those concerned with church growth, they are a rich mine of information.

Both men observed that the poor were quite adept at exploiting overgenerous churches. Some would go from one church or chapel to the next for the various handouts on offer at the time. If expected to attend church to receive their handout, they would do so—for that occasion alone. Even when they admired the work of a particular church, it would occur to very few that this might encourage them to become involved in worship themselves. As much as Booth and Rowntree admired, for example, the work of the Salvation Army, neither of them were convinced that it did much for local churchgoing.

As Quakers, neither of them were particularly fond of Roman Catholicism. Unsympathetic remarks about the papacy and about priestly authority punctuate Booth's accounts particularly. Nevertheless, both he and Rowntree observed that Catholics behaved quite differently from most other denominations in deprived urban areas. Catholics demanded from the poor as much as they gave to them. Priests were themselves poor and they depended on the poor, and the poor in return came to their churches.

All of this suggests that mission and care should not be confused. I believe that their common link is in worship. Worship requires mission and worship also requires care in the community. If worship is fully valued by churches, then mission becomes an imperative. It should be important for Christians to wish to share their worship with as many other people as possible. If worship invites people to move beyond self-regarding interest, then it should also encourage them to go out to care for others.

The right hand and the left hand of worship—the one hand concerned with mission and the other with care—connected by the body, our worship of God in Christ.

If there were only mission and no care, then the

critics of church growth would surely be right, it would simply be a question of numbers—or, if you prefer, 'bums on seats'. Forget about the quality, it is quantity that matters. That, though, would hardly be an adequate understanding of the church.

Quality *does* matter and care is, indeed, about quality. Selfless care cannot be used to promote something else; it is selfless. Real care can be costly. It is undertaken simply as a response to the God of love that we encounter in worship—that and nothing else. Real care is Christ-like. The way of the Cross is all about care beyond self-regarding interest.

There is much evidence that many still yearn for real communities and for abiding values even in pluralist Britain today. Confident secularity is not the only ideology that abounds. Churches can be responsive to these yearnings. They offer enduring communities that are harbingers of abiding values. Few other organizations or bodies in society are so richly endowed.

Of course, there are quite a number of communities in modern Britain carrying values—sometimes values deeply at odds with Christian values. Joyriders, typically, belong to tightly knit communities, as do delinquent gangs in many parts of the world. They have their own moral codes and sanctions—if only to protect each other from a hostile world. They may not believe in other people's property rights, but they are strongly committed to group loyalty. Betraying a mate would be deeply iniquitous.

Wars of aggression can also foster communities with strong values. Political dictators and tyrants have always known this. A war of aggression can bind people together into a single moral community

—a community determined to crush its enemies and even to conquer the world.

Churches certainly do not have the monopoly on moral communities. What they offer, instead, are communities that have been moulded over centuries and are bearers of abiding, Christ-like values. Even while admitting our weaknesses, Christian communities carry within them the resources to change, to forgive and be forgiven, and to become more Christ-like.

There is another irony here. Christians are frequently accused by others of being less than Christian in our behaviour. Recently, some strident secular voices have denounced Christianity because of the evil it has caused the world. Yet, even these denunciations often reflect the very Christian values that are being denounced. Their very moral outrage seems to presume that there really *are* abiding values in the world. Despite all the rhetoric, moral stridency makes most sense if this really *is* a world created by a loving God.

Critics of Christianity often depend on the values of Christianity in order to make their criticisms. Ironic as this is, it does illustrate my final point. Churches that cease to be pelicans will be concerned to spread their values deeply into society at large. If pelicans are content to be oddities within society, churches should not be. The Gospel requires us to seek to change the world—both to care for the world and to spill our values into the world.

In a pluralist society, there are many opportunities to do just that. A previous generation of Christians in Britain tended to assume that they were working towards a Christian society. Our present generation

113

is tempted, instead, to believe that society is deeply secular and that, increasingly, Christians will need to withdraw from society.

In contrast, I believe that society is deeply confused and that, despite considerable pluralism, many people yearn for more abiding values. Churches could respond more readily to these yearnings. Even if society itself might never become fully Christian, it can still be shaped by Christian values. In reality, Christian values and assumptions still permeate British society at many levels.

EPILOGUE

Ending with God

The pelican has begun to disappear. Once he was always there in Psalm 102. Modern translations tend to replace him with more vague talk about 'a wild bird' or just 'a bird'. Perhaps pelicans could also disappear from churches.

Part of the trouble is that most British churches have been declining for so long. Even when we talk optimistically, denominations as a whole still manage to decline. Churchgoing figures hold steady one year, so there is excitement that the tide has begun to turn, and people feel that there is no need to do anything differently—churches will start to fill again of their own accord. Then, the following year, church-going figures are down again. It is not too difficult to see how decline becomes a way of life. That is just how things are.

What I have tried to show in this book is that things do not have to be that way at all. No one should underestimate the size of the problem. Britain is not South-East Asia. Our population is not booming and many people have become apathetic about Christianity, even if the values they hold are often derived from it. However much people might yearn for real communities or for abiding values, they have yet to yearn for the churches.

Increasingly, children lack any effective Christian education in Britain today. So, to add to the problem of apathy from older people, there is sheer ignorance to contend with from the young. Resonances that might exist for older people are simply unfamiliar or even alien to many young people.

Growth will be achieved only with vision and radical action. It demands strategy as well as faith.

It would be wrong, though, to end with the subject of strategy. I have suggested many different ways that both denominations and local congregations could plan for growth. This needs a clear head, honesty, and a willingness to test and retest. If a particular plan does not produce growth, then admit as much, and try another plan. Keep trying, keep being honest, and keep testing. That is how dynamic bodies grow, even in difficult times.

In the end, however, it is a vision of God that must guide our actions. Let me end with a vision of a church for the future.

This church will be effective in sharing worship, and the effects of worship, with others. Faith in God, expressed through a renewed worship and structures for worship, might yet empower more people to live a Christian life in the twenty-first century than it has in the late twentieth century.

This church will be determined to draw as many people as possible into its worship in the belief that this worship is the primary and most distinctive way that we sustain our relationship to God the creator and redeemer of all that is.

This church will seek to mould human lives, to help people to live for others and, thus, become more Christ-like in their lives.

This church will locate both care and mission in

worship—worship offered to the God who loves and sustains us beyond anything that we deserve.

If long-term decline has been the experience of most British denominations, the hints offered here suggest that this decline might not be the irresistible force it was once thought to be. There are things that churches can do—if we have the courage and the will. We can leave the pelicans where they belong—in the wilderness—and become a church more able to lead people gently back to God.